Three Plays by
Edward Albee

Three Plays by
Edward Albee

The Death of Bessie Smith
The Sandbox
The American Dream

OVERLOOK DUCKWORTH
New York • London

This edition first published in the United States and the UK in 2013 by
Overlook Duckworth, Peter Mayer Publishers, Inc.
New York and London

NEW YORK:
141 Wooster Street
New York, NY 10012
www.overlookpress.com
For bulk and special sales, please contact sales@overlookny.com,
or write us at the above address

LONDON:
Gerald Duckworth & Co. Ltd.
30 Calvin Street
London E1 6NW
info@duckworth-publishers.co.uk
www.ducknet.co.uk

Cataloging-in-Publication Data is available from the Library of Congress

Book design and type formatting by Bernard Schleifer
Manufactured in the United States of America
1 3 5 7 9 8 6 4 2
ISBN 978-1-4683-0338-4 US
ISBN 978-0-7156-4532-1 UK

Contents

The Death of Bessie Smith

A PLAY IN EIGHT SCENES

For Ned Rorem

FIRST PERFORMANCE

April 21, 1960, Berlin, Germany.
Schlosspark Theater

The first American performance of *The Death of Bessie Smith* was presented at the York Playhouse in New York City on January 24, 1961.

THE PLAYERS

BERNIE
A Negro, about forty, thin.

JACK
A dark-skinned Negro, forty-five, bulky, with a deep voice and a mustache.

THE FATHER
A thin, balding white man, about fifty-five.

THE NURSE
A Southern white girl, full blown, dark or red-haired, pretty, with a wild laugh. Twenty-six.

THE ORDERLY
A light-skinned Negro, twenty-eight, clean-shaven, trim, prim.

SECOND NURSE
A Southern white girl, blond, not too pretty, about thirty.

THE INTERN
A Southern white man, blond, well put-together, with an amiable face; thirty.

THE SCENE

Afternoon and early evening, September 26, 1937. In and around the city of Memphis, Tennessee.

THE SET

The set for this play will vary, naturally, as stages vary—from theatre to theatre. So, the suggestions put down below, while they might serve as a useful guide, are but a general idea—what the author "sees."

What the author "sees" is this: The central and front area of the stage reserved for the admissions room of a hospital, for this is where the major portion of the action of the play takes place. The admissions desk and chair stage-center, facing the audience. A door, leading outside, stage-right; a door, leading to further areas of the hospital, stage-left. Very little more: a bench, perhaps; a chair or two. Running along the rear of the stage, and perhaps a bit on the sides, there should be a raised platform, on which, at various locations, against just the most minimal suggestions of sets, the other scenes of the play are performed. All of this very open, for the whole back wall of the stage is full of the sky, which will vary from scene to scene: a hot blue; a sunset; a great, red-orange-yellow sunset. Sometimes full, sometimes but a hint.

At the curtain, let the entire stage be dark against the sky, which is a hot blue. MUSIC *against this, for a moment or so, fading to under as the lights come up on:*

SCENE ONE

The corner of a barroom. BERNIE *seated at a table, a beer before him, with glass.* JACK *enters, tentatively, a beer bottle in his hand; he does not see* BERNIE.

BERNIE

(Recognizing JACK; *with pleased surprise)* Hey!

JACK

Hm?

BERNIE

Hey; Jack!

JACK

Hm? . . . What? . . . *(Recognizes him)* Bernie!

BERNIE

What you doin' here, boy? C'mon, sit down.

JACK

Well, I'll be damned . . .

BERNIE

C'mon, sit down, Jack.

JACK

Yeah . . . sure . . . well, I'll be damned. *(Moves over to the table; sits)* Bernie. My God, it's hot. How you been, boy?

BERNIE

Fine; fine. What you *doin'* here?

JACK

Oh, travelin'; travelin'.

BERNIE

On the move, hunh? Boy, you are the last person I expected t'walk in that door; small world, hunh?

JACK

Yeah; yeah.

BERNIE

On the move, hunh? Where you goin'?

JACK

(Almost, but not quite, mysterious) North.

BERNIE *(Laughs)*

North! North? That's a big place, friend: north.

JACK

Yeah . . . yeah, it is that: a big place.

BERNIE

(After a pause; laughs again) Well, *where,* boy? North *where?*

JACK

(Coyly; proudly) New York.

BERNIE

New York!

JACK

Unh-hunh; unh-hunh.

BERNIE

New York, hunh? Well. What you got goin' up there?

JACK

(Coy again) Oh . . . well . . . I got somethin' goin' up there. What *you* been up to, boy?

BERNIE

New York, hunh?

JACK

(Obviously dying to tell about it) Unh-hunh.

BERNIE

(Knowing it) Well, now, isn't that somethin'. Hey! You want a beer? You want another beer?

JACK

No, I gotta get . . . well, I don't know, I . . .

BERNIE

(Rising from the table) Sure you do. Hot like this? You need a beer or two, cool you off.

JACK

(*Settling back*) Yeah; why not? Sure, Bernie.

BERNIE

(*A dollar bill in his hand; moving off*) I'll get us a pair. New York, hunh? What's it all about, Jack? Hunh?

JACK (*Chuckles*)

Ah, you'd be surprised, boy; you'd be surprised.

(*Lights fade on this scene, come up on another, which is*)

SCENE TWO

Part of a screened-in porch; some wicker furniture, a little the worse for wear.

The NURSE's FATHER *is seated on the porch, a cane by his chair. Music, loud, from a phonograph, inside.*

FATHER

(*The music is too loud; he grips the arms of his chair; finally*) Stop it! Stop it! Stop it! Stop it!

NURSE (*From inside*)

What? What did you say?

FATHER

STOP IT!

NURSE

(*Appearing, dressed for duty*) I can't hear you; what do you want?

FATHER

Turn it off! Turn that goddamn music off!

NURSE

Honestly, Father . . .

FATHER

Turn it off!

(*The* NURSE *turns wearily, goes back inside. Music stops*)

Goddamn Nigger records. (*To* NURSE, *inside*) I got a headache.

NURSE *(Re-entering)*
What?

FATHER
I said, I got a headache; you play those goddamn records all the time; blast my head off; you play those goddamn Nigger records full blast . . . me with a headache . . .

NURSE *(Wearily)*
You take your pill?

FATHER
No!

NURSE *(Turning)*
I'll get you your pills. . . .

FATHER
I don't want 'em!

NURSE *(Overpatiently)*
All right; then I won't get you your pills.

FATHER
(After a pause; quietly, petulantly) You play those goddamn records all the time. . . .

NURSE *(Impatiently)*
I'm sorry, Father; I didn't know you had your headache.

FATHER
Don't you use that tone with me!

NURSE
(With that tone) I wasn't using any tone . . .

FATHER
Don't argue!

NURSE
I am not arguing; I don't *want* to argue; it's too *hot* to argue. *(Pause; then quietly)* I don't see why a person can't play a couple of records around here without . . .

FATHER
Damn noise! That's all it is; damn noise.

NURSE

(*After a pause*) I don't suppose you'll drive me to work. I don't suppose, with your headache, you feel up to driving me to the hospital.

FATHER

No.

NURSE

I didn't think you would. And I suppose *you're* going to need the car, too.

FATHER

Yes.

NURSE

Yes; I figured you would. What are you going to do, Father? Are you going to sit here all afternoon on the porch, with your headache, and *watch* the car? Are you going to sit here and watch it all afternoon? You going to sit here with a shotgun and make sure the birds don't crap on it . . . or something?

FATHER

I'm going to need it.

NURSE

Yeah; sure.

FATHER

I said, I'm going to need it.

NURSE

Yeah . . . I heard you. You're going to need it.

FATHER

I am!

NURSE

Yeah; no doubt. You going to drive down to the Democratic Club, and sit around with that bunch of loafers? You going to play big politician today? Hunh?

FATHER

That's enough, now.

NURSE

You going to go down there with that bunch of bums . . . light up one of those expensive cigars, which you have no business smoking, which you can't afford, which *I* cannot afford, to put it more accurately . . . the same brand His Honor the mayor smokes . . . you going to sit down there and talk big, about how you and the mayor are like *this* . . . you going to pretend you're something more than you really are, which is nothing but . . .

FATHER

You be quiet, you!

NURSE

. . . a hanger-on . . . a flunky . . .

FATHER

YOU BE QUIET!

NURSE *(Faster)*

Is that what you need the car for, Father, and I am going to have to take that hot, stinking bus to the hospital?

FATHER

I said, quiet! *(Pause)* I'm sick and tired of hearing you disparage my friendship with the mayor.

NURSE *(Contemptuous)*

Friendship!

FATHER

That's right: friendship.

NURSE

I'll tell you what I'll do: Now that we have His Honor, the mayor, as a patient . . . when I get down to the hospital . . . if I ever get there on that damn bus . . . I'll pay him a call, and I'll just *ask* him about your "friendship" with him; I'll just . . .

FATHER

Don't you go disturbing him; you hear me?

NURSE

Why, I should think the mayor would be *delighted* if the daughter of one of his closest friends was to . . .

FATHER

You're going to make trouble!

NURSE *(Heavily sarcastic)*

Oh, how could I make trouble, Father?

FATHER

You be careful.

NURSE

Oh, that must be quite a friendship. Hey, I got a good idea: you could drive me down to the hospital and you could pay a visit to your good friend the mayor at the same time. Now, *that* is a good idea.

FATHER

Leave off! Just leave off!

NURSE

(Under her breath) You make me sick.

FATHER

What! What was that?

NURSE *(Very quietly)*

I said, you make me sick, Father.

FATHER

Yeah? Yeah?
(He takes his cane, raps it against the floor several times. This gesture, beginning in anger, alters, as it becomes weaker, to a helpless and pathetic flailing; eventually it subsides; the NURSE *watches it all quietly)*

NURSE *(Tenderly)*

Are you done?

FATHER

Go away; go to work.

NURSE

I'll get you your pills before I go.

FATHER *(Tonelessly)*

I said, I don't want them.

NURSE

I don't care whether you *want* them, or not. . . .

FATHER

I'm not one of your patients!

NURSE

Oh, and aren't I glad you're not.

FATHER
You give them better attention than you give me!

NURSE *(Wearily)*
I don't have patients, Father; I am not a floor nurse; will you get that into your head? I am on admissions; I am on the admissions desk. You *know* that; why do you pretend otherwise?

FATHER
If you were a . . . what-do-you-call-it . . . if you were a floor nurse . . . if you *were*, you'd give your patients better attention than you give me.

NURSE
'What *are* you, Father? What are you? Are you sick, or not? Are you a . . . a . . . a poor cripple, or are you planning to get yourself up out of that chair, after I go to work, and drive yourself down to the Democratic Club and sit around with that bunch of loafers? Make up your mind, Father; you can't have it every which way.

FATHER
Never mind.

NURSE
You can't; you just can't.

FATHER
Never mind, now!

NURSE
(After a pause) Well, I gotta get to work.

FATHER *(Sneering)*
Why don't you get your boyfriend to drive you to work?

NURSE
All right; leave off.

FATHER
Why don't you get him to come by and pick you up, hunh?

NURSE
I said, leave off!

FATHER
Or is he only interested in driving you back here at night . . . when it's nice and dark; when it's plenty dark for messing around in his

car? Is that it? Why don't you bring him here and let *me* have a look
at him; why don't you let me get a look at him some time?

NURSE *(Angry)*
Well, Father . . . *(A very brief gesture at the surroundings)* maybe
it's because I don't want him to get a . . .

FATHER
I hear you; I hear you at night; I hear you gigglin' and carrying on
out there in his car; I hear you!

NURSE
(Loud; to cover the sound of his voice) I'm going, Father.

FATHER
All right; get along, then; get on!

NURSE
You're damned right!

FATHER
Go on! Go!
    (The NURSE *regards him for a moment; turns, exits)*
And don't stay out there all night in his car, when you get back. You
hear me? *(Pause)* You hear me?
    (Lights fade on this scene; come up on)

SCENE THREE

A bare area. JACK *enters, addresses his remarks off stage
and to an invisible mirror on an invisible dresser. Music
under this scene, as though coming from a distance.*

JACK
Hey . . . Bessie! C'mon, now. Hey . . . honey? Get your butt out of bed
. . . wake up. C'mon; the goddamn afternoon's half gone; we gotta get
movin'. Hey . . . I called that son-of-a-bitch in New York . . . *I* told him,
all right. I told him what you said. Wake up, baby, we gotta get out
of this dump; I gotta get you to Memphis 'fore seven o'clock . . . and
then . . . POW! . . . *we* are headin' straight north. Here we come; NEW
YORK. I told that bastard . . . I said: Look, you don't have no exclu-

sive rights on Bessie . . . nobody's got 'em . . . Bessie is doin' you a
favor . . . she's doin' you a goddamn favor. She don't *have* to sing for
you. I said: Bessie's tired . . . she don't wanna travel now. An' he said:
You don't *wanna* back out of this . . . Bessie told me *herself* . . . and
I said: Look . . . don't worry yourself . . . Bessie said she'd cut more
sides for you . . . she will . . . she'll make all the goddamn new records
you want. . . . What I mean to say *is*, just don't you get any ideas
about havin' exclusive rights . . . because nobody's got 'em. *(Giggles)*
I told him you was free as a bird, honey. Free as a goddamn bird.
(Looks in at her, shakes his head) Some bird! I been downstairs to
check us out. I go downstairs to check us out, and I run into a friend
of mine . . . and we sit in the bar and have a few, and he says: What're
you doin' now; what're you doin' in this crummy hotel? And I say: I
am cartin' a bird around with me. I'm cartin' her north; I got a fat
lady upstairs; she is sleepin' off last night. An' he says: You always got
some fat lady upstairs, somewhere; boy, I never seen it fail. An' I say:
This ain't just no plain fat lady I got upstairs . . . this is a celebrity,
boy . . . this is a rich old fat singin' lady . . . an' he laughed an' he said:
Boy, who you got up there? I say: You guess. An' he says: C'mon . . .
I can't *guess*. An' I told him . . . I am travelin' with Miss Bessie Smith.
An' he looked at me, an' he said, real quiet: Jesus, boy, are you travelin' with Bessie? An' I said . . . an' real proud: You're damn right I'm
travelin' with Bessie. An' he wants to meet you; so you get your big
self out of bed; we're goin' to go downstairs, 'cause I wanna show
you off. C'mon, now; I mean I *gotta* show you off. 'Cause then he
said: Whatever *happened* to Bessie? An' I said: What do you mean,
whatever happened to Bessie? She's right upstairs. An' he said: I
mean, what's she been doin' the past four-five years? There was a
time there, boy, Chicago an' all, New York, she was the hottest goddamn thing goin'. Is she still singin'? YOU HEAR THAT? That's
what he said: Is she still singin'? An' I said . . . I said, you been tired
. . . you been restin'. You ain't been forgotten, honey, but they are
askin' questions. SO YOU GET UP! We're drivin' north tonight, an'
when you get in New York . . . *you* show 'em where you been. Honey,
you're gonna go back on top again . . . I mean it . . . you *are*. I'm gonna
get you up to New York. 'Cause you gotta make that date. I mean,
sure, baby, you're free as a goddamn bird, an' I did tell that son-of-
a-bitch he don't have exclusive rights on you . . . but, honey . . . he *is*
interested . . . an' you gotta hustle for it now. You do; 'cause if you
don't do *somethin'*, people are gonna stop askin' where you been the

past four-five years . . . they're gonna stop askin' anything at all! You
hear? An' if I say downstairs you're rich . . . that don't make it so,
Bessie. No more, honey. You gotta make this goddamn trip . . . you
gotta get goin' again. *(Pleading)* Baby? Honey? You know I'm not
lyin' to you. C'mon now; get up. We go downstairs to the bar an'
have a few . . . see my friend . . . an' then we'll get in that car . . . and
go. 'Cause it's gettin' late, honey . . . it's gettin' awful late. *(Brighter)*
Hey! You awake? *(Moving to the wings)* Well, c'mon, then, Bessie
. . . let's get up. We're goin' north again!

(The lights fade on this scene.

Music.

The sunset is predominant)

JACK'S VOICE

Ha, ha; thanks; thanks a lot. *(Car door slams. Car motor starts)*
O.K.; here we go; we're on our way. *(Sound of car motor gunning,
car moving off, fading)*

(The sunset dims again.

Music, fading, as the lights come up on)

SCENE FOUR

The admissions room of the hospital. The NURSE *is at her
desk; the* ORDERLY *stands to one side.*

ORDERLY

The mayor of Memphis! I went into his room and there he was; the
mayor of Memphis. Lying right there, flat on his belly . . . a cigar in
his mouth . . . an unlit cigar stuck in his mouth, chewing on it, chewing on a big, unlit cigar . . . shuffling a lot of papers in his hands, a
pillow shoved up under his chest to give him some freedom for all
those papers . . . and I came in, and I said: Good afternoon, Your
Honor . . . and he swung his face 'round and he looked at me and he
shouted: My ass hurts, you get the hell out of here!

NURSE *(Laughs freely)*

His Honor has got his ass in a sling, and that's for sure.

ORDERLY

And I got out; I left very quickly; I closed the door fast.

NURSE

The mayor and his hemorrhoids . . . the mayor's late hemorrhoids . . . are a matter of deep concern to this institution, for the mayor built this hospital; the mayor is here with his ass in a sling, and the seat of government is now in Room 206 . . . so you be nice and respectful. (*Laughs*) There is a man two rooms down who walked in here last night after you went off . . . that man walked in here with his hands over his gut to keep his insides from spilling right out on this desk . . .

ORDERLY

I heard. . . .

NURSE

. . . and that man may live, or he may not live, and the wagers are heavy that he will not live . . . but we are not one bit more concerned for that man than we are for His Honor . . . no sir.

ORDERLY (*Chuckling*)

I like your contempt.

NURSE

You what? You like my *contempt*, do you? Well now, don't misunderstand me. Just what do you think I meant? What have you got it in your mind that I was saying?

ORDERLY

Why, it's a matter of proportion. Surely you don't *condone* the fact that the mayor and his piles, and that poor man lying up there . . . ?

NURSE

Condone! Will you listen to that: condone! My! Aren't you the educated one? What . . . what does that word mean, boy? That word condone? Hunh? You do talk some, don't you? You have a great deal to learn. Now it's true that the poor man lying up there with his guts coming out could be a Nigger for all the attention he'd get if His Honor should start shouting for something . . . he could be on the operating table . . . and they'd drop his insides right on the floor and come running if the mayor should want his cigar lit. . . . But that is the way things *are*. Those are facts. You had better acquaint yourself with some realities.

ORDERLY

I know . . . I know the mayor is an important man. He is impressive
. . . even lying on his belly like he is. . . . I'd like to get to talk to him.

NURSE

Don't you know it! TALK to him! Talk to the mayor? What for?

ORDERLY

I've told you. I've told you I don't intend to stay here carrying crap
pans and washing out the operating theatre until I have a . . . a long
gray beard . . . I'm . . . I'm going beyond that.

NURSE *(Patronizing)*

Sure.

ORDERLY

I've told you . . . I'm going beyond that. This . . .

NURSE

(Shakes her head in amused disbelief) Oh, my. Listen . . . you should
count yourself lucky, boy. Just what do you think is going to happen
to you? Is His Honor, the mayor, going to rise up out of his sickbed
and take a personal interest in you? Write a letter to the President,
maybe? And is Mr. Roosevelt going to send his wife, Lady Eleanor,
down here after you? Or is it in your plans that you are going to be
handed a big fat scholarship somewhere to the north of Johns
Hopkins? Boy, you just don't know! I'll tell you something . . . you
are lucky as you are. Whatever do you expect?

ORDERLY

What's been promised. . . . Nothing more. Just that.

NURSE

Promised! Promised? Oh, boy, I'll tell you about promises. Don't
you know yet that everything is promises . . . and that is all there is
to it? Promises . . . nothing more! I am personally sick of promises.
Would you like to hear a little poem? Would you like me to recite
some verse for you? Here is a little poem: "You kiss the Niggers and
I'll kiss the Jews and we'll stay in the White House as long as we
choose." And that . . . according to what I am told . . . that is what
Mr. and Mrs. Roosevelt sit at the breakfast table and sing to each
other over their orange juice, right in the White House. Promises,
boy! Promises . . . and that is what they are going to stay.

ORDERLY

There are *some* people who believe in more than promises. . . .

NURSE

Hunh?

ORDERLY *(Cautious now)*

I say, there are some people who believe in more than promises; there are some people who believe in action.

NURSE

What's that? What did you say?

ORDERLY

Action . . . ac— . . . Never mind.

NURSE *(Her eyes narrow)*

No . . . no, go on now . . . action? What kind of action do you mean?

ORDERLY

I don't *mean* anything . . . all I said was . . .

NURSE

I heard you. You know . . . I know what you been doing. You been listening to the great white doctor again . . . that big, good-looking blond intern you *admire* so much because he is so liberal-thinking, eh? My suitor? *(Laughs)* My suitor . . . my very own white knight, who is wasting his time patching up decent folk right here when there is dying going on in Spain. *(Exaggerated)* Oh, there is dying in Spain. And he is held here! That's who you have been listening to.

ORDERLY

I don't mean that. . . . I don't pay any attention . . . *(Weakly)* to that kind of talk. I do my job here . . . I try to keep . . .

NURSE *(Contemptuous)*

You try to keep yourself on the good side of everybody, don't you, boy? You stand there and you nod your kinky little head and say yes'm, yes'm, at everything I say, and then when he's here you go off in a corner and you get him and you sympathize with him . . . you get him to tell you about . . . promises! . . . and . . . and . . . action! . . . I'll tell you right now, he's going to get himself into trouble . . . and you're helping him right along.

ORDERLY

No, now. I don't . . .

NURSE *(With some disgust)*

All that talk of his! Action! I know all what he talks about . . . like about that bunch of radicals came through here last spring . . . causing the rioting . . . that arson! Stuff like that. Didn't . . . didn't you have someone get banged up in that?

· ORDERLY *(Contained)*

My uncle got run down by a lorry full of state police . . .

NURSE

. . . which the Governor called out because of the rioting . . . and that arson! Action! That was a fine bunch of action. Is that what you mean? Is that what you get him off in a corner and get him to talk about . . . and pretend you're interested? Listen, boy . . . if you're going to get yourself in with those folks, you'd better . . .

ORDERLY *(Quickly)*

I'm not mixed up with any folks . . . honestly . . . I'm not. I just want to . . .

NURSE

I'll tell you what you just want. . . . I'll tell you what you just want if you have any mind to keep this good job you've got. . . . You just shut your ears . . . and you keep that mouth closed tight, too. All this talk about what you are going to go beyond! You keep walking a real tight line here, and . . . and at night . . . *(She begins to giggle)* . . . and at night, if you want to, on your own time . . . at night you keep right on putting that bleach on your hands and your neck and your face . . .

ORDERLY

I do no such thing!

NURSE *(In full laughter)*

. . . and you keep right on bleaching away . . . b-l-e-a-c-h-i-n-g a-w-a-y . . . but you do that on your own time . . . you can do all that on your own time.

ORDERLY *(Pleading)*

I do no such thing!

NURSE

The hell you don't! You are such a . . .

ORDERLY

That kind of talk is very . . .

NURSE

. . . you are so mixed up! You are going to be one funny sight. You, over there in a corner playing up to him . . . well, boy, you are going to be one funny sight come the millennium. . . . The great black mob marching down the street, banners in the air . . . that great black mob . . . and you right there in the middle, your bleached-out, snowy-white face in the middle of the pack like that . . . *(She breaks down in laughter)* . . . oh . . . oh, my . . . oh. I tell you, that will be quite a sight.

ORDERLY *(Plaintive)*

I wish you'd stop that.

NURSE

Quite a sight.

ORDERLY

I wish you wouldn't make fun of me . . . I don't give you any cause.

NURSE

Oh, my . . . oh, I *am* sorry . . . I am *so* sorry.

ORDERLY

I don't think I give you any cause. . . .

NURSE

You don't, eh?

ORDERLY

No.

NURSE

Well . . . you *are* a true little gentleman, that's for sure . . . you *are* polite . . . and deferential . . . and you are a genuine little ass-licker, if I ever saw one. Tell me, boy . . .

ORDERLY

(Stiffening a little) There is no need . . .

NURSE

(Maliciously solicitous) Tell me, boy . . . is it true that you have Uncle Tom'd yourself right out of the bosom of your family . . . right out of your circle of acquaintances? Is it true, young man, that you are now an inhabitant of no-man's-land, on the one side shunned and dis-

owned by your brethren, and on the other an object of contempt and derision to your betters? Is that your problem, son?

ORDERLY

You . . . you shouldn't do that. I . . . work hard . . . I try to advance myself . . . I give nobody trouble.

NURSE

I'll tell you what you do. . . . You go north, boy . . . you go up to New York City, where nobody's any better than anybody else . . . get up north, boy. *(Abrupt change of tone)* But before you do anything like that, you run on downstairs and get me a pack of cigarettes.

ORDERLY

(Pauses. Is about to speak; thinks better of it; moves off to door, rear) Yes'm.

(Exits)

NURSE

(Watches him leave. After he is gone, shakes her head, laughs, parodies him)

Yes'm . . . yes'm . . . ha, ha, ha! You white Niggers kill me.

(She picks up her desk phone, dials a number, as the lights come up on)

SCENE FIVE

Which is both the hospital set of the preceding scene and, as well, on the raised platform, another admissions desk of another hospital. The desk is empty. The phone rings, twice. The SECOND NURSE *comes in, slowly, filing her nails, maybe.*

SECOND NURSE

(Lazily answering the phone) Mercy Hospital.

NURSE

Mercy Hospital! Mercy, indeed, you away from your desk all the time. *Some* hospitals are run better than *others; some* nurses stay at their posts.

SECOND NURSE *(Bored)*

Oh, hi. What do you want?

NURSE

I don't *want* anything. . . .

SECOND NURSE

(Pause) Oh. Well, what did you call for?

NURSE

I didn't call *for* anything. I *(Shrugs)* just called.

SECOND NURSE

Oh.

> *(The lights dim a little on the two nurses. Music. Car sounds up)*

JACK'S VOICE

(Laughs) I tell you, honey, he didn't like that. No, sir, he didn't. You comfortable, honey. Hunh? You just lean back and enjoy the ride, baby; we're makin' good time. Yes, we are makin' . . . WATCH OUT! WATCH . . .

> *(Sound of crash. . . . Silence)*

Honey . . . baby . . . we have crashed . . . you all right? . . . BESSIE! BESSIE!

> *(Music up again, fading as the lights come up full again on the two nurses)*

NURSE

. . . and, what else? Oh, yeah; *we* have got the mayor here.

SECOND NURSE

That's nice. What's he doin'?

NURSE

He isn't *doin'* anything; he is a patient here.

SECOND NURSE

Oh. Well, *we* had the mayor's wife *here* . . . last April.

NURSE

Unh-hunh. Well, *we* got the mayor *here*, now.

SECOND NURSE *(Very bored)*

Unh-hunh. Well, that's nice.

NURSE

(Turns, sees the INTERN *entering)* Oh, lover-boy just walked in; I'll call you later, hunh?

SECOND NURSE

Unh-hunh.

(They both hang up. The lights fade on the SECOND NURSE*)*

SCENE SIX

NURSE

Well, how is the Great White Doctor this evening?

INTERN *(Irritable)*

Oh . . . drop it.

NURSE

Oh, my . . . where is your cheerful demeanor this evening, Doctor?

INTERN

(Smiling in spite of himself) How do you do it? How do you manage to just dismiss things from your mind? How can you say a . . . cheerful hello to someone . . . dismissing from your mind . . . excusing yourself for the vile things you have said the evening before?

NURSE *(Lightly)*

I said nothing vile. I put you in your place . . . that's all. I . . . I merely put you in your place . . . as I have done before . . . and as I shall do again.

INTERN

(Is about to say something; thinks better of it; sighs) Never mind . . . forget about it . . . Did you *see* the sunset?

NURSE *(Mimicking)*

No, I didn't *see* the sunset. *What* is it doing?

INTERN

(Amused. Puts it on heavily) The west is burning . . . fire has enveloped fully half of the continent . . . the . . . the fingers of the flame stretch upward to the stars . . . and . . . and there is a monstrous burning circumference hanging on the edge of the world.

NURSE *(Laughs)*

Oh, my . . . oh, my.

INTERN *(Serious)*

It's a truly beautiful sight. Go out and have a look.

NURSE *(Coquettish)*

Oh, Doctor, I am chained to my desk of pain, so I must rely on you. . . . Talk the sunset to me, you . . . you monstrous burning intern hanging on the edge of my circumference . . . ha, ha, *ha.*

INTERN

(Leans toward her) When?

NURSE

When?

INTERN *(Lightly)*

When . . . when are you going to let me nearer, woman?

NURSE

Oh, my!

INTERN

Here am I . . . here am I tangential, while all the while I would serve more nobly as a radiant, not outward from, but reversed, plunging straight to your lovely vortex.

NURSE *(Laughs)*

Oh, la! You must keep your mind off my lovely vortex . . . you just remain . . . uh . . . tangential.

INTERN *(Mock despair)*

How is a man to fulfill himself? Here I offer you love . . . consider the word . . . love. . . . Here I offer you my love, my self . . . my bored bed . . .

NURSE

I note your offer . . . your offer is noted. *(Holds out a clipboard)* Here . . . do you want your reports?

INTERN

No . . . I don't want my reports. Give them here. *(Takes the clipboard)*

NURSE

And while you're here with your hot breath on me, hand me a cigarette. I sent the Nigger down for a pack. I ran out. *(He gives her a cigarette)* Match?

INTERN

Go light it on the sunset. *(Tosses match to her)* He says you owe him for three packs.

NURSE

(*Lights her cigarette*) Your bored bed . . . indeed.

INTERN

Ma'am . . . the heart yearns, the body burns . . .

NURSE

And *I* haven't time for *in*terns.

INTERN

. . . the heart yearns, the body burns . . . and I haven't time . . . Oh,
I don't know . . . the things you women can do to art.

(*More intimate, but still light*)

Have you told your father, yet? Have you told your father that I am
hopelessly in love with you? Have you told him that at night the sheets
of my bed are like a tent, poled center-upward in my love for you?

NURSE (*Wry*)

I'll tell him . . . I'll tell my father just that . . . just what you said . . . and
he'll be down here after you for talking to a young lady like that! Really!

INTERN

My God! I forgot myself! A cloistered maiden in whose house
trousers are never mentioned . . . in which flies, I am sure, are referred
to only as winged bugs. Here I thought I was talking to someone, to
a certain young nurse, whose collection of anatomical jokes for all
occasions . . .

NURSE (*Giggles*)

Oh, you be still, now. (*Lofty*) Besides, just because I play coarse and
flip around here . . . to keep my place with the rest of you . . . don't
you think for a minute that I relish this turn to the particular from
the general. . . . If you don't mind, we'll just cease this talk.

INTERN (*Half sung*)

I'm always in tumescence for you. You'd never guess the things I . . .

NURSE (*Blush-giggle*)

Now stop that! Really, I mean it!

INTERN

Then marry me, woman. If nothing else, marry me.

NURSE

Don't, now.

INTERN

(*Joking and serious at the same time*) Marry me.

NURSE

(*Matter-of-fact, but not unkindly*) I am sick of this talk. My poor father may have some funny ideas; he may be having a pretty hard time reconciling himself to things as they are. But not me! Forty-six dollars a month! Isn't that right? Isn't that what you make? Forty-six dollars a month! Boy, you can't afford even to think about marrying. You can't afford marriage. . . . Best you can afford is lust. That's the best you can afford.

INTERN (*Scathing*)

Oh . . . gentle woman . . . nineteenth-century lady out of place in this vulgar time . . . maiden versed in petit point and murmured talk of the weather . . .

NURSE

Now I mean it . . . you can cut that talk right out.

INTERN

. . . type my great-grandfather fought and died for . . . forty-six dollars a month and the best I can afford is lust! Jesus, woman!

NURSE

All right . . . you can quit making fun of me. You can quit it right this minute.

INTERN

I! Making fun of *you* . . . !

NURSE

I am tired of being toyed with; I am tired of your impractical propositions. Must you dwell on what is not going to happen? Must you ask me, constantly, over and over again, the same question to which you are already aware you will get the same answer? Do you get pleasure from it? What unreasonable form of contentment do you derive from persisting in this?

INTERN (*Lightly*)

Because I love you?

NURSE

Oh, that would help matters along; it really would . . . even if it were *true.* The economic realities would pick up their skirts, whoop, and depart before the lance-high, love-smit knight. My knight, whose real and true interest, if we come right down to it, as indicated in the order of your propositions, is, and always has been, a convenient and uncomplicated bedding down.

INTERN
(Smiling, and with great gallantry) I have offered to marry you.

NURSE
Yeah . . . sure . . . you have offered to marry me. The United States is chuck-full of girls who have heard that great promise—I will marry you . . . I will marry you . . . IF! If! The great promise with its great conditional attached to it. . . .

INTERN *(Amused)*
Who are you pretending to be?

NURSE *(Abrupt)*
What do you mean?

INTERN *(Laughing)*
Oh, *nothing.*

NURSE
(Regards him silently for a moment; then) Marry me! Do you know . . . do you know that Nigger I sent to fetch me a pack of butts . . . do you know he is in a far better position . . . realistically, economically . . . to ask to marry me than you are? Hunh? Do you know that? That Nigger! Do you know that Nigger outearns you . . . and by a *lot?*

INTERN
(Bows to her) I know he does . . . and I know what value you, you and your famous family, put on such things. So, I have an idea for you . . . why don't you just *ask* that Nigger to marry you? 'Cause, boy, he'd never ask you! I'm sure if you told your father about it, it would give him some pause at first, because we know what type of man your father is . . . don't we? . . . But then he would think about it . . . and realize the advantages of the match . . . realistically . . . economically . . . and he would find some way to adjust his values, in consideration of your happiness, and security. . . .

NURSE
(Flicks her still-lit cigarette at him, hard; hits him with it) You are disgusting!

INTERN

Damn you, bitch!

NURSE

Disgusting!

INTERN

Realistic . . . practical . . . (*A little softer, now*) Your family is a famous *name*, but those thousand acres are *gone*, and the pillars of your house are blistered and flaking . . . (*Harder*) Not that your family ever *had*, within human memory, a thousand acres to *go* . . . *or* a house with pillars in the first place. . . .

NURSE (*Angry*)

I am fully aware of what is true and what is not true. (*Soberly*) Go about your work and leave me be.

INTERN (*Sweetly*)

Aw.

NURSE

I said . . . leave me be.

INTERN

(*Brushing himself*) It is a criminal offense to set fire to interns . . . orderlies you may burn at will, unless you have other plans for them . . . but interns . . .

NURSE

. . . are a dime a dozen. (*Giggles*) Did I burn you?

INTERN

No, you did not burn me.

NURSE

That's too bad . . . would have served you right if I had. (*Pauses; then smiles*) I'm sorry, honey.

INTERN (*Mock formal*)

I accept your apology . . . and I await your surrender.

NURSE (*Laughs*)

Well, you just await it. (*A pause*) Hey, what are you going to do about the mayor being here now?

INTERN

What am I supposed to do about it? I am on emergencies, and he is not an emergency case.

NURSE

I told you . . . I told you what you should do.

INTERN

I know . . . I should go upstairs to his room . . . I should pull up a chair, and I should sit down and I should say, How's tricks, Your Honor?

NURSE

Well, you make fun if you want to . . . but if you listen to me, you'll know you need some people *behind* you.

INTERN

Strangers!

NURSE

Strangers don't stay strangers . . . not if you don't let them. He could do something for you if he had a mind to.

INTERN

Yes he could . . . indeed, he *could* do something for me. . . . He could give me his car . . . he could make me a present of his Cord automobile. . . . That would be the finest thing any mayor ever did for a private citizen. Have you seen that car?

NURSE

Have I seen that car? Have I seen this . . . have I seen that? Cord automobiles and . . . and sunsets . . . those are . . . fine preoccupations. Is that what you think about? Huh? Driving a fine car into a fine sunset?

INTERN (*Quietly*)

Lord knows, I'd like to get away from here.

NURSE (*Nodding*)

I know . . . I know. Well, maybe you're going to *have* to get away from here. People are aware how dissatisfied you are . . . people have heard a lot about your . . . dissatisfaction. . . . My father has heard . . . people got wind of the way you feel about things. People here aren't good enough for your attentions. . . . Foreigners . . . a bunch of foreigners who are cutting each other up in their own business . . . that's where you'd like to be, isn't it?

INTERN (*Quietly; intensely*)

There are over half a million people killed in that war! Do you know that? By airplanes. . . . Civilians! You misunderstand me so! I am . . . all right . . . this way. . . . My dissatisfactions . . . you call them that . . . my dissatisfactions have nothing to do with loyalties. . . . I am not concerned with politics . . . but I have a sense of urgency . . . a dislike of waste . . . stagnation . . . I am *stranded . . . here*. . . . My talents are not large . . . but the emergencies of the emergency ward of this second-rate hospital in this second-rate state . . . No! . . . it isn't enough. Oh, you listen to me. If I could . . . if I could bandage the arm of one person . . . if I could be over there right this minute . . . you could take the city of Memphis . . . you could take the whole state . . . and don't you forget I was born here . . . you could take the whole goddamn state. . . .

NURSE *(Hard)*

Well, I have a very good idea of how we could arrange that. I have a dandy idea. . . . We could just tell the mayor about the way you feel, and he'd be delighted to help you on your way . . . out of this hospital at the very least, and maybe out of the state! And I don't think he'd be giving you any Cord automobile as a going-away present, either. He'd set you out, all right . . . he'd set you right out on your *butt!* That's what he'd do.

INTERN

(With a rueful half-smile) Yes . . . yes . . . I imagine he would. I feel lucky . . . I feel doubly fortunate, now . . . having you . . . feeling the way we do about each other.

NURSE

You are so sarcastic!

INTERN

Well, how the hell do you expect me to behave?

NURSE

Just . . . *(Laughs)* . . . oh, boy, this is good . . . just like I told the Nigger . . . you walk a straight line, and you do your job . . . *(Turns coy, here)* . . . and . . . and unless you are kept late by some emergency more pressing than your . . . *(Smiles wryly)* . . . "love" . . . for me . . . I may let you drive me home tonight . . . in your beat-up Chevy.

INTERN

Woman, as always I anticipate with enormous pleasure the prospect of driving you home . . . a stop along the way . . . fifteen minutes or so . . . of tantalizing preliminary love play ending in an infuriating and inconclusive wrestling match, during which you hiss of the . . . the liberties I should not take, and I sound the horn once or twice accidentally with my elbow . . .

(She giggles at this)

. . . and finally, in my beat-up car, in front of your father's beat-up house . . . a kiss of searing intensity . . . a hand in the right place . . . briefly . . . and your hasty departure within. I am looking forward to this ritual . . . as I always do.

NURSE *(Pleased)*

Why, thank you.

INTERN

I look forward to this ritual because of how it sets me apart from other men . . .

NURSE

Aw . . .

INTERN

. . . because I am probably the only white man under sixty in two counties who has *not* had the pleasure of . . .

NURSE

LIAR! You no-account mother-grabbing son of a Nigger!

INTERN *(Laughs)*

Boy! Watch you go!

NURSE

FILTH! You are filth!

INTERN

I am honest . . . an honest man. Let me make you an honest woman.

NURSE

(Steaming . . . her rage between her teeth) You have done it, boy . . . you have played around with me and you have done it. I am going to get you. . . . I am going to fix you . . . I am going to see to it that you are *through* here . . . do you understand what I'm telling you?

INTERN

There is no ambiguity in your talk now, honey.

NURSE

You're damn right there isn't.

(The ORDERLY *re-enters from stage-rear. The* NURSE *sees him)*

Get out of here!

(*But he stands there*)

Do you hear me? You get the hell out of here! GO!

(*He retreats, exits, to silence*)

INTERN (*Chuckling*)

King of the castle. My, you *are* something.

NURSE

Did you get what I was telling you?

INTERN

Why, I heard every word . . . every sweet syllable. . . .

NURSE

You have overstepped yourself . . . and you are going to wish you hadn't. I'll get my father . . . I'll have you done with *myself*

INTERN (*Cautious*)

Aw, come on, now.

NURSE

I mean it.

INTERN (*Lying badly*)

Now look . . . you don't think I meant . . .

NURSE (*Mimicking*)

Now you don't think I meant . . . (*Laughs broadly*) Oh, my . . . you are the funny one.

(*Her threat, now, has no fury, but is filled with quiet conviction*)

I said I'll fix you . . . and I will. You just go along with your work . . . you do your job . . . but what I said . . . you keep that burning in the back of your brain. We'll go right along, you and I, and we'll be civil . . . and it'll be as though nothing had happened . . . nothing at all. (*Laughs again*) Honey, your neck is in the *noose* . . . and I have a whip . . . and I'll set the horse from under you . . . when it pleases me.

INTERN (*Wryly*)

It's going to be nice around here.

NURSE

Oh, yes it is. I'm going to enjoy it . . . I really am.

INTERN

Well. . . I'll forget about driving you home tonight. . . .

NURSE

Oh, no . . . you will *not* forget about driving me home tonight. You will drive me home *tonight* . . . you will drive me home *tonight* . . . and *tomorrow* night . . . you will see me to my *door* . . . you will be my gallant. We will have things between us a little bit the way I am told things *used* to be. You will *court* me, boy, and you will do it *right!*

INTERN

(Stares at her for a moment) You impress me. No matter what else, I've got to admit that.

> *(The* NURSE *laughs wildly at this. Music. The lights on this hospital set fade, and come up on the* SECOND NURSE, *at her desk, for)*

SCENE SEVEN

JACK

(Rushing in) Ma'am, I need help, quick!

SECOND NURSE

What d'you want here?

JACK

There has been an accident, ma'am . . . I got an injured woman outside in my car. . . .

SECOND NURSE

Yeah? Is that so? Well, you sit down and wait. . . . You go over there and sit down and wait a while.

JACK

This is an emergency! There has been an accident!

SECOND NURSE

YOU WAIT! You just sit down and wait!

JACK

This woman is badly . . .

SECOND NURSE

YOU COOL YOUR HEELS!

JACK

Ma'am . . . I got Bessie Smith out in that car there. . . .

SECOND NURSE

I DONT CARE WHO YOU GOT OUT THERE, NIGGER. YOU
COOL YOUR HEELS!

(*Music up.*

*The lights fade on this scene, come up again on the main
hospital scene, on the* NURSE *and the* INTERN, *for*)

SCENE EIGHT

(*Music fades*)

NURSE (*Loud*)

Hey, Nigger . . . Nigger!

(*The* ORDERLY *re-enters*)

Give me my cigarettes.

INTERN

I think I'll . . .

NURSE

You stay here!

(*The* ORDERLY *hands the nurse the cigarettes, cautious and
attentive to see what is wrong*)

A person could die for a smoke, the time you take. What'd you do . . .
sit downstairs in the can and rest your small, shapely feet . . . hunh?

ORDERLY

You told me to . . . go back outside . . .

NURSE

Before that! What'd you do . . . go to the cigarette *factory?* Did you take a quick run up to Winston-Salem for these?

ORDERLY

No . . . I . . .

NURSE

Skip it. *(To the* INTERN*)* Where? Where were you planning to go?

INTERN *(Too formal)*

I beg your pardon?

NURSE

I said . . . where did you want to go to? Were you off for coffee?

INTERN

Is that what you want? Now that you have your cigarettes, have you hit upon the idea of having coffee, too? Now that he is back from one errand, are you planning to send me on another?

NURSE *(Smiling wickedly)*

Yeah . . . I think I'd like that . . . keep both of you jumping. I *would* like coffee, and I *would* like you to get it for me. So why don't you just trot right across the hall and get me some? And I like it good and hot . . . and strong . . .

INTERN

. . . and black . . . ?

NURSE

Cream! . . . and sweet . . . and in a hurry!

INTERN

I guess your wish is my command . . . hunh?

NURSE

You bet it is!

INTERN

(Moves halfway to the door, stage-rear, then pauses)

I just had a lovely thought . . . that maybe sometime when you are sitting there at your desk opening mail with that stiletto you use for a letter opener, you might slip and tear open your arm . . . then you could come running into the emergency . . . and I could be there when you came running in, blood coming out of you like water out of a faucet . . . and I could take ahold of your arm . . . and just hold it . . . just hold it . . . and watch it flow . . . just hold on to you and watch your blood flow . . .

NURSE
(Grabs up the letter opener . . . holds it up)
This? More likely between your ribs!

INTERN *(Exiting)*
One coffee, lady.

NURSE
(After a moment of silence, throws the letter opener back down onher desk)
I'll take care of him. CRACK! I'll crack that whip. *(To the* ORDERLY*)* What are you standing there for . . . hunh? You like to watch what's going on?

ORDERLY
I'm no voyeur.

NURSE
You what? You like to listen in? You take pleasure in it?

ORDERLY
I said no.

NURSE *(Half to herself)*
I'll bet you don't. I'll take care of him . . . talking to me like that . . . I'll crack that whip. Let him just wait.

(To the ORDERLY, *now)*
My father says that Francisco Franco is going to be victorious in that war over there . . . that he's going to win . . . and that it's just wonderful.

ORDERLY
He does?

NURSE
Yes, he does. My father says that Francisco Franco has got them licked, and that they're a bunch of radicals, anyway, and it's all to the good . . . just wonderful.

ORDERLY
Is that so?

NURSE

I've told you my father is a . . . a historian, so he isn't just anybody. His opinion counts for something special. It *still* counts for something special. He says anybody wants to go over there and get mixed up in that thing has got it coming to him . . . whatever happens.

ORDERLY

I'm sure your father is an informed man, and . . .

NURSE

What?

ORDERLY

I said . . . I said . . . I'm sure your father is an informed man, and . . . his opinion is to be respected.

NURSE

That's right, boy . . . you just jump to it and say what you think people want to hear . . . you be both sides of the coin. Did you . . . did you hear him threaten me there? Did you?

ORDERLY

Oh, now . . . I don't think . . .

NURSE *(Steely)*

You heard him threaten me!

ORDERLY

I don't think . . .

NURSE

For such a smart boy . . . you are so dumb. I don't know what I am going to do with you.

   (She is thinking of the INTERN *now, and her expression shows it)*

You refuse to comprehend things and that bodes badly . . . it does. Especially considering it is all but arranged . . .

ORDERLY

What is all but arranged?

NURSE

   (A great laugh, but mirthless. She is barely under control)

Why, don't you know, boy? Didn't you know that you and I are practically engaged?

ORDERLY

I . . . I don't . . .

NURSE

Don't you know about the economic realities? Haven't you been appraised of the way things *are? (She giggles)* Our knights are gone forth into sunsets . . . behind the wheels of Cord cars . . . the acres have diminished and the paint is flaking . . . that there is a great . . . *abandonment?*

ORDERLY *(Cautious)*

I don't understand you . . .

NURSE

No kidding? (Her *voice shakes*) No kidding . . . you don't understand me? Why? What's the matter, boy, don't you get the idea?

ORDERLY *(Contained, but angry)*

I think you'd tire of riding me some day. I think you *would* . . .

NURSE

You go up to Room 206, right now . . . you go up and tell the mayor that when his butt's better we have a marrying job for him.

ORDERLY *(With some distaste)*

Really . . . you go much too far. . . .

NURSE

Oh, I do, do I? Well, let me tell you something . . . I am sick of it! I am *sick*. I am sick of everything in this hot, stupid, fly-ridden *world*. I am sick of the disparity between things as they are, and as they should be! I am sick of this desk . . . this uniform . . . it scratches. . . . I am sick of the sight of *you* . . . the *thought* of you makes me . . . *itch*. . . . I am sick of *him. (Soft now: a chant)* I am sick of talking to people on the phone in this damn stupid hospital. . . . I am sick of the smell of Lysol . . . I could die of it. . . . I am sick of going to bed and I am sick of waking up. . . . I am tired . . . I am tired of the truth . . . and I am tired of lying about the truth . . . I am tired of my skin. . . . I WANT OUT!

ORDERLY

(After a short pause) Why don't you go into emergency . . . and lie down?

   (He approaches her)

NURSE

Keep away from me.

(At this moment the outside door bursts open and JACK *plunges into the room. He is all these things: drunk, shocked, frightened. His face should be cut, but no longer bleeding. His clothes should be dirtied . . . and in some disarray. He pauses, a few steps into the room, breathing hard)*

NURSE

Whoa! Hold on there, you.

ORDERLY *(Not advancing)*

What do you want?

JACK

(After more hard breathing; confused) What . . . ?

NURSE

You come banging in through that door like that? What's the matter with you? *(To the* ORDERLY*)* Go see what's the matter with him.

ORDERLY *(Advancing slightly)*

What do you *want?*

JACK *(Very confused)*

What do I want . . . ?

ORDERLY *(Backing off)*

You can't come in here like this . . . banging your way in here . . . don't you know any better?

NURSE

You drunk?

JACK

(Taken aback by the irrelevance) I've been drinking . . . yes . . . all right . . . I'm drunk. *(Intense)* I got someone outside . . .

NURSE

You stop that yelling. This is a white hospital, you.

ORDERLY *(Nearer the* NURSE*)*

That's right. She's right. This is a private hospital . . . a semi-private hospital. If you go on . . . into the city . . .

JACK *(Shakes his head)*

No. . . .

NURSE

Now you listen to me, and you get this straight . . . *(Pauses just perceptibly, then says the word, but with no special emphasis)* . . . Nigger . . . this is a semiprivate white hospital . . .

JACK *(Defiant)*

I don't care!

NURSE

Well, you *get* on. . . .

ORDERLY

(As the INTERN *re-enters with two containers of coffee)*

You go on now . . . you go . . .

INTERN

What's all this about?

ORDERLY

I told him to go on into Memphis . . .

INTERN

Be quiet. *(To* JACK*)* What is all this about?

JACK

Please . . . I got a woman . . .

NURSE

You been told to move on.

INTERN

You got a woman . . .

JACK

Outside . . . in the car. . . . There was an accident . . . there is blood. . . . Her arm . . .

INTERN

(After thinking for a moment, looking at the NURSE, *moves toward the outside door)*

All right . . . we'll go see. *(To the* ORDERLY, *who hangs back)* Come on, you . . . let's go.

ORDERLY

(*Looks to the* NURSE) We told him to go on into Memphis.

NURSE

(*To the* INTERN, *her eyes narrowing*) Don't you go out there!

INTERN

(*Ignoring her; to the* ORDERLY) You heard me . . . come on!

NURSE (*Strong*)

I told you . . . DON'T GO OUT THERE!

INTERN (*Softly, sadly*)

Honey . . . you going to fix me? You going to have the mayor throw me out of here on my butt? Or are you going to arrange it in Washington to have me *deported*? What *are* you going to do . . . hunh?

NURSE (*Between her teeth*)

Don't go out there . . .

INTERN

Well, honey, whatever it is you're going to do . . . it might as well be now as any other time.

(*He and the* ORDERLY *move to the outside door*)

NURSE

(*Half angry, half plaintive, as they exit*)

Don't go!

(*After they exit*)

I warn you! I *will* fix you. You go out that door . . . you're through here.

(JACK *moves to a vacant area near the bench, stage-right.*
The NURSE *lights a cigarette*)

I told you I'd fix you . . . I'll fix you. (*Now, to* JACK) I think I said this was a white hospital.

JACK (*Wearily*)

I know, lady . . . you told me.

NURSE

(*Her attention on the door*) You don't have sense enough to do what you're told . . . you make trouble for yourself . . . you make trouble for other people.

JACK (*Sighing*)

I don't care . . .

NURSE

You'll care!

JACK

(*Softly, shaking his head*) No . . . I won't care. (*Now, half to her, half to himself*) We were driving along . . . not very fast . . . I don't think we were driving fast . . . we were in a hurry, yes . . . and I had been drinking . . . *we* had been drinking . . . but I *don't* think we were driving fast . . . not too fast . . .

NURSE

(*Her speeches now are soft comments on his*)
. . . driving drunk on the road . . . it not even dark yet . . .

JACK

. . . but then there was a car . . . I hadn't seen it . . . it couldn't have seen me . . . from a side road . . . hard, fast, sudden . . . (*Stiffens*) . . . CRASH! (*Loosens*) . . . and we weren't thrown . . . both of us . . . both cars stayed on the road . . . but we were stopped . . . my motor, running. . . . I turned it off . . . the door . . . the right door was all smashed in. . . . That's all it was . . . no more damage than that . . . but we had been riding along . . . laughing . . . it was cool driving, but it was warm out . . . and she had her arm out the window . . .

NURSE

. . . serves you right . . . drinking on the road . . .

JACK

. . . and I said . . . I said, Honey, we have crashed . . . you all right? (*His face contorts*) And I looked . . . and the door was all pushed in . . . she was caught there . . . where the door had pushed in . . . her right side, crushed into the torn door, the door crushed into her right side. . . . BESSIE! BESSIE! . . . (*More to the* NURSE, *now*) . . . but ma'am . . . her arm . . . her right arm . . . was torn off . . . almost torn off from her shoulder . . . and there was blood . . . SHE WAS BLEEDING SO . . . !

NURSE (*From a distance*)

Like water from a faucet . . . ? Oh, that is terrible . . . terrible . . .

JACK

I didn't wait for nothin' . . . the other people. . . the other car . . . I
started up . . . I started . . .

NURSE *(More alert)*

You took *off?* . . . You took off from an accident?

JACK

Her arm, ma'am . . .

NURSE

You probably got police looking for you right now . . . you know that?

JACK

Yes, ma'am . . . I suppose so . . . and I drove . . . there was a hospital about a mile up . . .

NURSE

(Snapping to attention) THERE! You went somewhere *else?* You
been somewhere else already? What are you doing *here* with that
woman then, hunh?

JACK

At the hospital . . . I came in to the desk and I told them what had
happened . . . and they said, you sit down and wait . . . you go over
there and sit down and wait a while. WAIT! It was a white hospital,
ma'am . . .

NURSE

This is a white hospital, too.

JACK

I said . . . this is an emergency . . . there has been an accident. . . . YOU
WAIT! You just sit down and wait. . . . I told them . . . I told them it
was an emergency . . . I said . . . this woman is badly hurt. . . . YOU
COOL YOUR HEELS! . . . I said, Ma'am, I got Bessie Smith out in
that car there . . . I DONT CARE WHO YOU GOT OUT THERE,
NIGGER . . . YOU COOL YOUR HEELS! . . . I couldn't wait there
. . . her in the car . . . so I left there . . . I drove on . . . I stopped on
the road and I was told where to come . . . and I came here.

NURSE *(Numb, distant)*

I know who she is . . . I heard her sing. *(Abruptly)* You give me your
name! You can't take off from an accident like that . . . I'll phone the
police; I'll tell them where you are!

(The INTERN *and the* ORDERLY *re-enter. Their uniforms are bloodied. The* ORDERLY *moves stage-rear, avoiding* JACK. *The intern moves in, staring at* JACK*)*

NURSE

He drove away from an accident . . . he just took off . . . and he didn't come right here, either . . . he's been to one hospital *already.* I *warned* you not to get mixed up in this. . . .

INTERN *(Softly)*

Shut up!

(Moves toward JACK, *stops in front of him)*

You tell me something . . .

NURSE

I warned you! You didn't listen to me . . .

JACK

You want my name, too . . . is that what you want?

INTERN

No, that's not what I want.

(He is contained, but there is a violent emotion inside him)

You tell me something. When you brought her here . . .

JACK

I brought her here . . . They wouldn't help her . . .

INTERN

All right. When you brought her here . . . when you brought this woman *here* . . .

NURSE

Oh, this is no plain woman . . . this is no ordinary Nigger . . . this is
    Bessie Smith!

INTERN

When you brought this woman *here* . . . when you drove up *here* . . . when you brought this woman *here* . . . DID YOU KNOW SHE WAS DEAD?

(Pause)

NURSE

Dead! . . . This Nigger brought a dead woman here?

INTERN

(Afraid of the answer) Well . . . ?

NURSE *(Distantly)*

Dead . . . dead.

JACK

(Wearily; turning, moving toward the outside door) Yes . . . I knew she was dead. She died on the way here.

NURSE

(Snapping to) Where you going? Where do you think you're going? I'm going to get the police here for you!

JACK

(At the door)

Just outside.

INTERN

(As JACK *exits)*

WHAT DID YOU EXPECT *ME* TO DO, EH? WHAT WAS *I* SUPPOSED TO DO?

*(*JACK *pauses for a moment, looks at him blankly, closes the door behind him)*

TELL ME! WHAT WAS I SUPPOSED TO DO?

NURSE *(Slyly)*

Maybe . . . maybe he thought you'd bring her back to life . . . great white doctor. *(Her laughter begins now, mounts to hysteria)* Great . . .white . . . doctor. . . . Where are you going to go now . . . great . . . white . . . doctor? You are finished. You have had your last patient here. . . . Off you go, boy! You have had your last patient . . . a Nigger . . . a dead Nigger lady . . . WHO SINGS. Well . . . I sing, too, boy . . . I sing real good. You want to hear me sing? Hunh? You want to hear the way I sing? HUNH?

(Here she begins to sing and laugh at the same time. The singing is tuneless, almost keening, and the laughter is almost crying)

INTERN

(Moves to her)

Stop that! Stop that!

(But she can't. Finally he slaps her hard across the face. Silence. She is frozen, with her hand to her face where he hit her. He backs toward the rear door)

ORDERLY

(His back to the wall)

I never heard of such a thing . . . bringing a dead woman here like that. . . . I don't know what people can be thinking of sometimes. . . .

(The INTERN *exits. The room fades into silhouette again. . . . The great sunset blazes; music up)*

CURTAIN

The Sandbox

A BRIEF PLAY, IN MEMORY OF MY

GRANDMOTHER (1876–1959)

The Sandbox was produced by Lion Associates at the Jazz Gallery in New York City on May 16, 1960. It was staged by Lawrence Arrick. Original music was composed by William Flanagan. The cast was as follows:

YOUNG MAN	Alan Helm
MOMMY	Jane Hoffman
DADDY	Richard Woods
GRANDMA	Sudie Bond
MUSICIAN	Hal McKusick

THE PLAYERS

THE YOUNG MAN

Twenty-five. A good-looking, well-built boy in a bathing suit.

MOMMY

Fifty-five. A well-dressed, imposing woman.

DADDY

Sixty. A small man; gray, thin.

GRANDMA

Eighty-six. A tiny, wizened woman with bright eyes.

THE MUSICIAN

No particular age, but young would be nice.

Note:

When, in the course of the play, MOMMY and DADDY call each other by these names, there should be no suggestion of regionalism. These names are of empty affection and point up the pre-senility and vacuity of their characters.

THE SCENE

A bare stage, with only the following: Near the foot-lights, far stage-right, two simple chairs set side by side, facing the audience; near the footlights, far stage-left, a chair facing stage-right with a music stand before it; far-ther back, and stage-center, slightly elevated and raked, a large child's sandbox with a toy pail and shovel; the background is the sky, which alters from brightest day to deepest night.

At the beginning, it is brightest day; the YOUNG MAN *is alone on stage, to the rear of the sandbox, and to one side. He is doing calisthenics; he does calisthenics until quite at the very end of the play. These calisthenics, employing the arms only, should suggest the beating and fluttering of wings. The* YOUNG MAN *is, after all, the Angel of Death.*

MOMMY *and* DADDY *enter from stage-left,* MOMMY *first.*

MOMMY

(Motioning to DADDY) Well, here we are; this is the beach.

DADDY *(Whining)*

I'm cold.

MOMMY

(Dismissing him with a little laugh) Don't be silly; it's as warm as toast. Look at that nice young man over there: *he* doesn't think it's cold. *(Waves to the* YOUNG MAN) Hello.

YOUNG MAN

(With an endearing smile) Hi!

MOMMY *(Looking about)*

This will do perfectly . . . don't you think so, Daddy? There's sand there . . . and the water beyond. What do you think, Daddy?

DADDY *(Vaguely)*

Whatever you say, Mommy.

MOMMY

(With the same little laugh) Well, of course . . . whatever I say. Then, it's settled, is it?

DADDY *(Shrugs)*

She's *your* mother, not mine.

MOMMY

I know she's my mother. What do you take me for? *(A pause)* All right, now; let's get on with it. *(She shouts into the wings, stage-left)* You! Out there! You can come in now.

(The MUSICIAN *enters, seats himself in the chair, stage-left, places music on the music stand, is ready to play.* MOMMY *nods approvingly)*

MOMMY

Very nice; very nice. Are you ready, Daddy? Let's go get Grandma.

DADDY
Whatever you say, Mommy.

MOMMY
(Leading the way out, stage-left) Of course, whatever I say. *(To the* MUSICIAN*)* You can begin now.

(The MUSICIAN *begins playing;* MOMMY *and* DADDY *exit; the* MUSICIAN, *all the while playing, nods to the* YOUNG MAN*)*

YOUNG MAN
(With the same endearing smile) Hi!

(After a moment, MOMMY *and* DADDY *re-enter, carrying* GRANDMA. *She is borne in by their hands under her armpits; she is quite rigid; her legs are drawn up; her feet do not touch the ground; the expression on her ancient face is that of puzzlement and fear)*

DADDY
Where do we put her?

MOMMY
(The same little laugh) Wherever I say, of course. Let me see . . . well . . . all right, over there . . . in the sandbox. *(Pause)* Well, what are you waiting for, Daddy? . . . The sandbox!

(Together they carry GRANDMA *over to the sandbox and more or less dump her in)*

GRANDMA
(Righting herself to a sitting position; her voice a cross between a baby's laugh and cry) Ahhhhhh! Graaaaa!

DADDY *(Dusting himself)*
What do we do now?

MOMMY
(To the MUSICIAN*)* You can stop now.

(The MUSICIAN *stops)*

(Back to DADDY*)* What do you mean, what do we do now? We go over there and sit down, of course. *(To the* YOUNG MAN*)* Hello there.

YOUNG MAN
(Again smiling) Hi!

(MOMMY *and* DADDY *move to the chairs, stage-right, and sit down. A pause*)

GRANDMA

(*Same as before*) Ahhhhhh! Ah-haaaaaa! Graaaaaa!

DADDY

Do you think . . . do you think she's . . . comfortable?

MOMMY (*Impatiently*)

How would I know?

DADDY

(*Pause*) What do we do now?

MOMMY

(*As if remembering*) We . . . wait. We . . . sit here . . . and we wait . . . that's what we do.

DADDY

(*After a pause*) Shall we talk to each other?

MOMMY

(*With that little laugh; picking something off her dress*) Well, *you* can talk, if you want to . . . if you can think of anything to *say* . . . if you can think of anything *new*.

DADDY (*Thinks*)

No . . . I suppose not.

MOMMY

(*With a triumphant laugh*) Of course not!

GRANDMA

(*Banging the toy shovel against the pail*) Haaaaaa! Ahhaaaaaa!

MOMMY

(*Out over the audience*) Be quiet, Grandma . . . just be quiet, and wait.

(GRANDMA *throws a shovelful of sand at* MOMMY)

MOMMY

(*Still out over the audience*) She's throwing sand at me! You stop that, Grandma; you stop throwing sand at Mommy! (*To* DADDY) She's throwing sand at me.

(DADDY *looks around at* GRANDMA, *who screams at him*)

GRANDMA

GRAAAAA!

MOMMY

Don't look at her. Just . . . sit here . . . be very still . . . and wait. (*To the* MUSICIAN) You . . . uh . . . you go ahead and do whatever it is you do.

(*The* MUSICIAN *plays*)

(MOMMY *and* DADDY *are fixed, staring out beyond the audience.* GRANDMA *looks at them, looks at the* MUSICIAN, *looks at the sandbox, throws down the shovel*)

GRANDMA

Ah-haaaaaa! Graaaaaa! (*Looks for reaction; gets none. Now . . . directly to the audience*) Honestly! What a way to treat an old woman! Drag her out of the house. . . stick her in a car . . . bring her out here from the city . . . dump her in a pile of sand . . . and leave her here to set. I'm eighty-six years old! I was married when I was seventeen. To a farmer. He died when I was thirty. (*To the* MUSICIAN) Will you stop that, please?

(*The* MUSICIAN *stops playing*)

I'm a feeble old woman . . . how do you expect anybody to hear me over that peep! peep! peep! (*To herself*) There's no respect around here. (*To the* YOUNG MAN) There's no respect around here!

YOUNG MAN

(*Same smile*) Hi!

GRANDMA

(*After a pause, a mild double-take, continues, to the audience*) My husband died when I was thirty (*indicates* MOMMY), and I had to raise that big cow over there all by my lonesome. You can imagine what *that* was like. Lordy! (*To the* YOUNG MAN) Where'd they get you?

YOUNG MAN

Oh . . . I've been around for a while.

GRANDMA

I'll bet you have! Heh, heh, heh. Will you look at you!

YOUNG MAN

(Flexing his muscles) Isn't that something? *(Continues his calisthenics)*

GRANDMA

Boy, oh boy; I'll say. Pretty good.

YOUNG MAN *(Sweetly)*

I'll say.

GRANDMA

Where ya from?

YOUNG MAN

Southern California.

GRANDMA *(Nodding)*

Figgers, figgers. What's your name, honey?

YOUNG MAN

I don't know. . . . .

GRANDMA

(To the audience) Bright, too!

YOUNG MAN

I mean . . . I mean, they haven't given me one yet . . . the studio . . .

GRANDMA

(Giving him the once-over) You don't say . . . you don't say. Well . . . uh, I've got to talk some more . . . don't you go 'way.

YOUNG MAN

Oh, no.

GRANDMA

(Turning her attention back to the audience) Fine; fine. *(Then, once more, back to the* YOUNG MAN*)* You're . . . you're an actor, huh?

YOUNG MAN *(Beaming)*

Yes. I am.

GRANDMA

(To the audience again; shrugs) I'm smart that way. *Anyhow,* I had to raise . . . *that* over there all by my lonesome; and what's next to her there . . . that's what she married. Rich? I tell you . . . money,

money, money. They took me off the *farm* . . . which was real decent
of them . . . and they moved me into the big town house with *them*
. . . fixed a nice place for me under the stove . . . gave me an army
blanket . . . and my own dish . . . my very own dish! So, what have I
got to complain about? Nothing, of course. I'm not complaining.
(She looks up at the sky, shouts to someone offstage) Shouldn't it be
getting dark now, dear?

> *(The lights dim; night comes on. The* MUSICIAN *begins to
> play; it becomes deepest night. There are spots on all the
> players, including the* YOUNG MAN, *who is, of course, con-
> tinuing his calisthenics)*

DADDY (Stirring)

It's nighttime.

MOMMY

Shhhh. Be still . . . wait.

DADDY (Whining)

It's so hot.

MOMMY

Shhhhhh. Be still . . . wait.

GRANDMA

(To herself) That's better. Night. *(To the* MUSICIAN*)* Honey, do you
play all through this part?

> *(The* MUSICIAN *nods)*

Well, keep it nice and soft; that's a good boy.

> *(The* MUSICIAN *nods again; plays softly)*

That's nice.

> *(There is an off-stage rumble)*

DADDY (Starting)

What was that?

MOMMY

(Beginning to weep) It was nothing.

DADDY

It was . . . it was . . . thunder . . . or a wave breaking . . . or something.

MOMMY

(Whispering, through her tears) It was an off-stage rumble and you know what *that* means. . . .

DADDY

I forget. . . .

MOMMY

(Barely able to talk) It means the time has come for poor Grandma . . . and I can't bear it!

DADDY *(Vacantly)*

I . . . I suppose you've got to be brave.

GRANDMA *(Mocking)*

That's right, kid; be brave. You'll bear up; you'll get over it.

(Another off-stage rumble . . . louder)

MOMMY

Ohhhhhhhhhh . . . poor Grandma . . . poor Grandma. . . .

GRANDMA *(To* MOMMY*)*

I'm fine! I'm all right! It hasn't happened yet!

(A violent off-stage rumble. All the lights go out, save the spot on the YOUNG MAN; *the* MUSICIAN *stops playing)*

MOMMY

Ohhhhhhhhhh . . . Ohhhhhhhhhh. . . .

(Silence)

GRANDMA

Don't put the lights up yet . . . I'm not ready; I'm not quite ready. *(Silence)* All right, dear . . . I'm about done.

(The lights come up again, to brightest day; the MUSICIAN *begins to play.* GRANDMA *is discovered, still in the sandbox, lying on her side, propped up on an elbow, half covered, busily shoveling sand over herself)*

GRANDMA *(Muttering)*

I don't know how I'm supposed to do anything with this goddamn toy shovel. . . .

DADDY

Mommy! It's daylight!

MOMMY (*Brightly*)

So it is! Well! Our long night is over. We must put away our tears, take off our mourning . . . and face the future. It's our duty.

GRANDMA

(*Still shoveling; mimicking*) . . . take off our mourning . . . face the future. . . . Lordy!

(MOMMY *and* DADDY *rise, stretch.* MOMMY *waves to the* YOUNG MAN)

YOUNG MAN

(*With that smile*) Hi!

(GRANDMA *plays dead.* (!) MOMMY *and* DADDY *go over to look at her; she is a little more than half buried in the sand; the toy shovel is in her hands, which are crossed on her breast*)

MOMMY

(*Before the sandbox; shaking her head*) Lovely! It's . . . it's hard to be sad . . . she looks . . . so happy. (*With pride and conviction*) It pays to do things well. (*To the* MUSICIAN) All right, you can stop now, if you want to. I mean, stay around for a swim, or something; it's all right with us. (*She sighs heavily*) Well, Daddy . . . off we go.

DADDY

Brave Mommy!

MOMMY

Brave Daddy!

(*They exit, stage-left*)

GRANDMA

(*After they leave; lying quite still*) It pays to do things well. . . . Boy, oh boy! (*She tries to sit up*) . . . well, kids . . . (*but she finds she can't*) . . . I . . . I can't get up. I . . . I can't move. . . .

(*The* YOUNG MAN *stops his calisthenics, nods to the* MUSICIAN, *walks over to* GRANDMA, *kneels down by the sandbox*)

GRANDMA

I . . . can't move. . . .

YOUNG MAN

Shhhhh . . . be very still. . . .

GRANDMA

I . . . I can't move. . . .

YOUNG MAN

Uh . . . ma'am; I . . . I have a line here.

GRANDMA

Oh, I'm sorry, sweetie; you go right ahead.

YOUNG MAN

I am . . . uh . . . I am . . .

GRANDMA

Take your time, dear.

YOUNG MAN

(*Prepares; delivers the line like a real amateur*) I am the Angel of Death. I am . . . uh . . . I am come for you.

GRANDMA

What . . . wha . . . (*Then, with resignation*) . . . ohhhh . . . ohhhh . . . I see.

> (*The* YOUNG MAN *bends over, kisses* GRANDMA *gently on the forehead*)

GRANDMA

(*Her eyes closed, her hands folded on her breast again, the shovel between her hands, a sweet smile on her face*)

Well . . . that was very nice, dear . . .

YOUNG MAN

(*Still kneeling*) Shhhhhh . . . be still. . . .

GRANDMA

What I meant was . . . you did that very well, dear. . . .

YOUNG MAN (*Blushing*)

. . . oh . . .

GRANDMA

No; I mean it. You've got that . . . you've got a quality.

YOUNG MAN

(*With his endearing smile*) Oh . . . thank you; thank you very much . . . ma'am.

GRANDMA

(Slowly; softly—as the YOUNG MAN *puts his hands on top of* GRAND-
MA's*)* You're . . . you're welcome . . . dear.

(Tableau. The MUSICIAN *continues to play as the curtain
slowly comes down)*

CURTAIN

The American Dream

A PLAY IN ONE SCENE

For David Diamond

The American Dream was first produced by Theatre 1961, Richard Barr and Clinton Wilder, at the York Playhouse, New York City, on January 24, 1961. It was directed by Alan Schneider. The sets and costumes were by William Ritman. The cast was as follows:

DADDY	John C. Becher
MOMMY	Jane Hoffman
GRANDMA	Sudie Bond
MRS. BARKER	Nancy Cushman
THE YOUNG MAN	Ben Piazza

THE PLAYERS

MOMMY

DADDY

GRANDMA

MRS. BARKER

YOUNG MAN

THE SCENE

A living room. Two armchairs, one toward either side of the stage, facing each other diagonally out toward the audience. Against the rear wall, a sofa. A door, leading out from the apartment, in the rear wall, far stage-right. An archway, leading to other rooms, in the side wall, stage-left.

At the beginning, MOMMY *and* DADDY *are seated in the arm-chairs,* DADDY *in the armchair stage-left,* MOMMY *in the other.*

Curtain up. A silence. Then:

MOMMY

I don't know what can be keeping them.

DADDY

They're late, naturally.

MOMMY

Of course, they're late; it never fails.

DADDY

That's the way things are today, and there's nothing you can do about it.

MOMMY

You're quite right.

DADDY

When we took this apartment, they were quick enough to have me sign the lease; they were quick enough to take my check for two months' rent in advance . . .

MOMMY

And one month's security . . .

DADDY

. . . and one month's security. They were quick enough to check my references; they were quick enough about all that. But now! But now, try to get the icebox fixed, try to get the doorbell fixed, try to get the leak in the johnny fixed! Just try it . . . they aren't so quick about *that.*

MOMMY

Of course not; it never fails. People think they can get away with anything these days . . . and, of course they can. I went to buy a new hat yesterday.

(Pause)

I said, I went to buy a new hat yesterday.

DADDY

Oh! Yes . . . yes.

MOMMY

Pay attention.

DADDY

I *am* paying attention, Mommy.

MOMMY

Well, be sure you do.

DADDY

Oh, I am.

MOMMY

All right, Daddy; now listen.

DADDY

I'm listening, Mommy.

MOMMY

You're sure!

DADDY

Yes . . . yes, I'm sure. I'm all ears.

MOMMY

(Giggles at the thought; then)

All right, now. I went to buy a new hat yesterday and I said, "I'd like a new hat, please." And so, they showed me a few hats, green ones and blue ones, and I didn't like any of them, not one bit. What did I say? What did I just say?

DADDY

You didn't like any of them, not one bit.

MOMMY

That's right; you just keep paying attention. And then they showed me one that I did like. It was a lovely little hat, and I said, "Oh, this is a lovely little hat; I'll take this hat; oh my, it's lovely. What color is it?" And they said, "Why, this is beige; isn't it a lovely little beige hat?" And I said, "Oh, it's just lovely." And so, I bought it.

(Stops, looks at DADDY)

DADDY

(To show he is paying attention)
And so you bought it.

MOMMY

And so I bought it, and I walked out of the store with the hat right on my head, and I ran spang into the chairman of our woman's club, and she said, "Oh, my dear, isn't that a lovely little hat? Where did you get that lovely little hat? It's the loveliest little hat; I've always wanted a wheat-colored hat *myself*" And, I said, "Why, no, my dear; this hat is beige; beige." And she laughed and said, "Why no, my dear, that's a wheat-colored hat . . . wheat. I know beige from wheat." And I said, "Well, my dear, I know beige from wheat, too." What did I say? What did I just say?

DADDY

(Tonelessly)
Well, my dear, I know beige from wheat, too.

MOMMY

That's right. And she laughed, and she said, "Well, my dear, they certainly put one over on you. That's wheat if I ever saw wheat. But it's lovely, just the same." And then she walked off. She's a dreadful woman, you don't know her; she has dreadful taste, two dreadful children, a dreadful house, and an absolutely adorable husband who sits in a wheelchair all the time. You don't know him. You don't know anybody, do you? She's just a dreadful woman, but she *is* chairman of our woman's club, so naturally I'm terribly fond of her. So, I went right back into the hat shop, and I said, "Look here; what do you mean selling me a hat that you say is beige, when it's wheat all the time . . . wheat! I can tell beige from wheat any day in the week, but not in this artificial light of yours." They have artificial light, Daddy.

DADDY

Have they!

MOMMY

And I said, "The minute I got outside I could tell that it wasn't a beige hat at all; it was a wheat hat." And they said to me, "How could you tell that when you had the hat on the top of your head?" Well, that made me angry, and so I made a scene right there; I screamed as hard as I could; I took my hat off and I threw it down on the

counter, and oh, I made a terrible scene. I said, I made a terrible
scene.

DADDY

(*Snapping to*)
Yes . . . yes . . . good for you!

MOMMY

And I made an absolutely terrible scene; and they became fright-
ened, and they said, "Oh, madam; oh, madam." But I kept right on,
and finally they admitted that they might have made a mistake; so
they took my hat into the back, and then they came out again with a
hat that looked exactly like it. I took one look at it, and I said, "This
hat is wheat-colored; wheat." Well, of course, they said, "Oh, no,
madam, this hat is beige; you go outside and see." So, I went outside,
and lo and behold, it *was* beige. So I bought it.

DADDY

(*Clearing his throat*)
I would imagine that it was the same hat they tried to sell you
before.

MOMMY

(*With a little laugh*)
Well, of course it was!

DADDY

That's the way things are today; you just can't get satisfaction; you
just try.

MOMMY

Well, *I* got satisfaction.

DADDY

That's right, Mommy. You *did* get satisfaction, didn't you?

MOMMY

Why are they so late? I don't know what can be keeping them.

DADDY

I've been trying for two weeks to have the leak in the johnny fixed.

MOMMY

You can't get satisfaction; just try. *I* can get satisfaction, but you can't.

DADDY

I've been trying for two weeks and it isn't so much for my sake; I can always go to the club.

'MOMMY

It isn't so much for my sake, either; I can always go shopping.

DADDY

It's really for Grandma's sake.

MOMMY

Of course it's for Grandma's sake. Grandma cries every time she goes to the johnny as it is; but now that it doesn't work it's even worse, it makes Grandma think she's getting feeble-headed.

DADDY

Grandma *is* getting feeble-headed.

MOMMY

Of course Grandma is getting feeble-headed, but not about her johnny-do's.

DADDY

No; that's true. I must have it fixed.

MOMMY

WHY are they so late? I don't know what can be keeping them.

DADDY

When they came here the first time, they were ten minutes early; they were quick enough about it then.

(*Enter* GRANDMA *from the archway, stage-left. She is loaded down with boxes, large and small, neatly wrapped and tied.*)

MOMMY

Why Grandma, look at you! What *is* all that you're carrying?

GRANDMA

They're boxes. What do they look like?

MOMMY

Daddy! Look at Grandma; look at all the boxes she's carrying!

DADDY

My goodness, Grandma; look at all those boxes.

GRANDMA

Where'll I put them?

MOMMY

Heavens! I don't know. Whatever are they for?

GRANDMA

That's nobody's damn business.

MOMMY

Well, in that case, put them down next to Daddy; there.

GRANDMA

(*Dumping the boxes down, on and around* DADDY's *feet*)
I sure wish you'd get the john fixed.

DADDY

Oh, I do wish they'd come and fix it. We hear you . . . for hours . . .
whimpering away. . . .

MOMMY

Daddy! What a terrible thing to say to Grandma!

GRANDMA

Yeah. For shame, talking to me that way.

DADDY

I'm sorry, Grandma.

MOMMY

Daddy's sorry, Grandma.

GRANDMA

Well, all right. In that case I'll go get the rest of the boxes. I suppose
I deserve being talked to that way. I've gotten so old. Most people
think that when you get so old, you either freeze to death, or you
burn up. But you don't. When you get so old, all that happens is that
people talk to you that way.

DADDY

(*Contrite*)
I said I'm sorry, Grandma.

MOMMY

Daddy said he was sorry.

GRANDMA

Well, that's all that counts. People being sorry. Makes you feel better; gives you a sense of dignity, and that's all that's important   a
sense of dignity. And it doesn't matter if you don't care, or not,
either. You got to have a sense of dignity, even if you don't care,
'cause, if you don't have that, civilization's doomed.

MOMMY

You've been reading my book club selections again!

DADDY

How dare you read Mommy's book club selections, Grandma!

GRANDMA

Because I'm old! When you're old you gotta do something. When
you get old, you can't talk to people because people snap at you.
When you get so old, people talk to you that way. That's why you
become deaf, so you won't be able to hear people talking to you
that way. And that's why you go and hide under the covers in the
big soft bed, so you won't feel the house shaking from people
talking to you that way. That's why old people die, eventually.
People talk to them that way. I've got to go and get the rest of the
boxes.

   (GRANDMA *exits*)

DADDY

Poor Grandma, I didn't mean to hurt her.

MOMMY

Don't you worry about it; Grandma doesn't know what she means.

DADDY

She knows what she says, though.

MOMMY

Don't you worry about it; she won't know that soon. I love Grandma.

DADDY

I love her, too. Look how nicely she wrapped these boxes.

MOMMY

Grandma has always wrapped boxes nicely. When I was a little girl,
I was very poor, and Grandma was very poor, too, because
Grandpa was in heaven. And every day, when I went to school,
Grandma used to wrap a box for me, and I used to take it with me

to school; and when it was lunchtime, all the little boys and girls used to take out their boxes of lunch, and they weren't wrapped nicely at all, and they used to open them and eat their chicken legs and chocolate cakes; and I used to say, "Oh, look at my lovely lunch box; it's so nicely wrapped it would break my heart to open it." And so, I wouldn't open it.

DADDY

Because it was empty.

MOMMY

Oh no. Grandma always filled it up, because she never ate the dinner she cooked the evening before; she gave me all her food for my lunch box the next day. After school, I'd take the box back to Grandma, and she'd open it and eat the chicken legs and chocolate cake that was inside. Grandma used to say, "I love day-old cake." That's where the expression day-old came from. Grandma always ate everything a day late. I used to eat all the other little boys' and girls' food at school, because they thought my lunch box was empty. They thought my lunch box was empty, and that's why I wouldn't open it. They thought I suffered from the sin of pride, and since that made them better than me, they were very generous.

DADDY

You were a very deceitful little girl.

MOMMY

We were very poor! But then I married you, Daddy, and now we're very rich.

DADDY

Grandma isn't rich.

MOMMY

No, but you've been so good to Grandma she feels rich. She doesn't know you'd like to put her in a nursing home.

DADDY

I wouldn't!

MOMMY

Well, heaven knows, *I* would! I can't stand it, watching her do the cooking and the housework, polishing the silver, moving the furniture. . . .

DADDY

She likes to do that. She says it's the least she can do to earn her keep.

MOMMY

Well, she's right. You can't live off people. I can live off you, because I married you. And aren't you lucky all I brought with me was Grandma. A lot of women I know would have brought their whole families to live off you. All I brought was Grandma. Grandma is all the family I have.

DADDY

I feel very fortunate.

MOMMY

You should. I have a right to live off of you because I married you, and because I used to let you get on top of me and bump your uglies; and I have a right to all your money when you die. And when you do, Grandma and I can live by ourselves . . . if she's still here. Unless you have her put away in a nursing home.

DADDY

I have no intention of putting her in a nursing home.

MOMMY

Well, I wish somebody would do something with her!

DADDY

At any rate, you're very well provided for.

MOMMY

You're my sweet Daddy; that's very nice.

DADDY

I love my Mommy.

(*Enter* GRANDMA *again, laden with more boxes*)

GRANDMA

(*Dumping the boxes on and around* DADDY's *feet*)
There; that's the lot of them.

DADDY

They're wrapped so nicely.

GRANDMA

(*To* DADDY)
You won't get on my sweet side that way . . .

MOMMY

Grandma!

GRANDMA

. . . telling me how nicely I wrap boxes. Not after what you said: how I whimpered for hours. . . .

MOMMY

Grandma!

GRANDMA

(To MOMMY*)*

Shut up!

(To DADDY*)*

You don't have any feelings, that's what's wrong with you. Old people make all sorts of noises, half of them they can't help. Old people whimper, and cry, and belch, and make great hollow rumbling sounds at the table; old people wake up in the middle of the night screaming, and find out they haven't even been asleep; and when old people *are* asleep, they try to wake up, and they can't . . . not for the longest time.

MOMMY

Homilies, homilies!

GRANDMA

And there's more, too.

DADDY

I'm really very sorry, Grandma.

GRANDMA

I know you are, Daddy; it's Mommy over there makes all the trouble. If you'd listened to me, you wouldn't have married her in the first place. She was a tramp and a trollop and a trull to boot, and she's no better now.

MOMMY

Grandma!

GRANDMA

(To MOMMY*)*

Shut up!

(To DADDY*)*

When she was no more than eight years old she used to climb up on my lap and say, in a sickening little voice, "When I gwo up, I'm going to mahwy a wich old man; I'm going to set my wittle were end right down in a tub o' butter, that's what I'm going to do." And I warned you, Daddy; I told you to stay away from her type. I told you to. I did.

MOMMY

You stop that! You're my mother, not his!

GRANDMA

I am?

DADDY

That's right, Grandma. Mommy's right.

GRANDMA

Well, how would you expect somebody as old as I am to remember a thing like that? You don't make allowances for people. I want an allowance. I want an allowance!

DADDY

All right, Grandma; I'll see to it.

MOMMY

Grandma! I'm ashamed of you.

GRANDMA

Humf! It's a fine time to say that. You should have gotten rid of me a long time ago if that's the way you feel. You should have had Daddy set me up in business somewhere . . . I could have gone into the fur business, or I could have been a singer. But no; not you. You wanted me around so you could sleep in my room when Daddy got fresh. But now it isn't important, because Daddy doesn't want to get fresh with you any more, and I don't blame him. You'd rather sleep with me, wouldn't you, Daddy?

MOMMY

Daddy doesn't want to sleep with anyone. Daddy's been sick.

DADDY

I've been sick. I don't even want to sleep in the apartment.

MOMMY

You see? I told you.

DADDY

I just want to get everything over with.

MOMMY

That's right. Why are they so late? Why can't they get here on time?

GRANDMA

(An owl)

Who? Who? . . . Who? Who?

MOMMY

You know, Grandma.

GRANDMA

No, I don't.

MOMMY

Well, it doesn't really matter whether you do or not.

DADDY

Is that true?

MOMMY

Oh, more or less. Look how pretty Grandma wrapped these boxes.

GRANDMA

I didn't really like wrapping them; it hurt my fingers, and it fright-ened me. But it had to be done.

MOMMY

Why, Grandma?

GRANDMA

None of your damn business.

MOMMY

Go to bed.

GRANDMA

I don't want to go to bed. I just got up. I want to stay here and watch. Besides . . .

MOMMY

Go to bed.

DADDY

Let her stay up, Mommy; it isn't noon yet.

GRANDMA

I want to watch; besides . . .

DADDY

Let her watch, Mommy.

MOMMY

Well all right, you can watch; but don't you dare say a word.

GRANDMA

Old people are very good at listening; old people don't like to talk; old people have colitis and lavender perfume. Now I'm going to be quiet.

DADDY

She never mentioned she wanted to be a singer.

MOMMY

Oh, I forgot to tell you, but it was ages ago.
  (The doorbell rings)
Oh, goodness! Here they are!

GRANDMA

Who? Who?

MOMMY

Oh, just some people.

GRANDMA

The van people? Is it the van people? Have you finally done it? Have you called the van people to come and take me away?

DADDY

Of course not, Grandma!

GRANDMA

Oh, don't be too sure. She'd have you carted off too, if she thought she could get away with it.

MOMMY

Pay no attention to her, Daddy.
  (An aside to GRANDMA*)*
My God, you're ungrateful!
  (The doorbell rings again)

DADDY

(Wringing his hands)
Oh dear; oh dear.

MOMMY

(Still to GRANDMA*)*
Just you wait; I'll fix your wagon.
(Now, to DADDY*)*
Well, go let them in, Daddy. What are you waiting for?

DADDY

I think we should talk about it some more. Maybe we've been hasty
. . . a little hasty, perhaps.
(Doorbell rings again)
I'd like to talk about it some more.

MOMMY

There's no need. You made up your mind; you were firm; you were
masculine and decisive.

DADDY

We might consider the pros and the . . .

MOMMY

I won't argue with you; it has to be done; you were right. Open the
door.

DADDY

But I'm not sure that . . .

MOMMY

Open the door.

DADDY

Was I firm about it?

MOMMY

Oh, so firm; so firm.

DADDY

And was I decisive?

MOMMY

SO decisive! Oh, I shivered.

DADDY

And masculine? Was I really masculine?

MOMMY

Oh, Daddy, you were so masculine; I shivered and fainted.

GRANDMA

Shivered and fainted, did she? Humf!

MOMMY

You be quiet.

GRANDMA

Old people have a right to talk to themselves; it doesn't hurt the gums, and it's comforting.
(Doorbell rings again)

DADDY

(Backing off from the door)
Maybe we can send them away.

MOMMY

Oh, look at you! You're turning into jelly; you're indecisive; you're a woman.

DADDY

All right. Watch me now; I'm going to open the door. Watch. Watch!

MOMMY

We're watching; we're watching.

GRANDMA

I'm not.

DADDY

Watch now; it's opening.
(He opens the door)
It's open!
(MRS. BARKER *steps into the room)*
Here they are!

MOMMY

Here they are!

GRANDMA

Where?

DADDY

Come in. You're late. But, of course, we expected you to be late; we were saying that we expected you to be late.

MOMMY

Daddy, don't be rude! We were saying that you just can't get satisfaction these days, and we were talking about you, of course. Won't you come in?

MRS. BARKER

Thank you. I don't mind if I do.

MOMMY

We're very glad that you're here, late as you are. You do remember us, don't you? You were here once before. I'm Mommy, and this is Daddy, and that's Grandma, doddering there in the corner.

MRS. BARKER

Hello, Mommy; hello, Daddy; and hello there, Grandma.

DADDY

Now that you're here, I don't suppose you could go away and maybe come back some other time.

MRS. BARKER

Oh no; we're much too efficient for that. I said, hello there, Grandma.

MOMMY

Speak to them, Grandma.

GRANDMA

I don't see them.

DADDY

For shame, Grandma; they're here.

MRS. BARKER

Yes, we're here, Grandma. I'm Mrs. Barker. I remember you; don't you remember me?

GRANDMA

I don't recall. Maybe you were younger, or something.

MOMMY

Grandma! What a terrible thing to say!

MRS. BARKER

Oh now, don't scold her, Mommy; for all she knows she may be right.

DADDY

Uh . . . Mrs. Barker, is it? Won't you sit down?

MRS. BARKER

I don't mind if I do.

MOMMY

Would you like a cigarette, and a drink, and would you like to cross your legs?

MRS. BARKER

You forget yourself, Mommy; I'm a professional woman. But I will cross my legs.

DADDY

Yes, make yourself comfortable.

MRS. BARKER

I don't mind if I do.

GRANDMA

Are they still here?

MOMMY

Be quiet, Grandma.

MRS. BARKER

Oh, we're still here. My, what an unattractive apartment you have!

MOMMY

Yes, but you don't know what a trouble it is. Let me tell you . . .

DADDY

I was saying to Mommy . . .

MRS. BARKER

Yes, I know. I was listening outside.

DADDY

About the icebox, and . . . the doorbell . . . and the . . .

MRS. BARKER

. . . and the johnny. Yes, we're very efficient; we have to know everything in our work.

DADDY

Exactly what do you do?

MOMMY

Yes, what is your work?

MRS. BARKER

Well, my dear, for one thing, I'm chairman of your woman's club.

MOMMY

Don't be ridiculous. I was talking to the chairman of my woman's club just yester— Why, so you are. You remember, Daddy, the lady I was telling you about? The lady with the husband who sits in the *swing?* Don't you remember?

DADDY

No . . . no . . .

MOMMY

Of course you do. I'm so sorry, Mrs. Barker. I would have known you anywhere, except in this artificial light. And look! You have a hat just like the one I bought yesterday.

MRS. BARKER

(With a little laugh)

No, not really; this hat is cream.

MOMMY

Well, my dear, that may look like a cream hat to you, but I can . . .

MRS. BARKER

Now, now; you seem to forget who I am.

MOMMY

Yes, I do, don't I? Are you sure you're comfortable? Won't you take off your dress?

MRS. BARKER

I don't mind if I do.

(She removes her dress)

MOMMY

There. You must feel a great deal more comfortable.

MRS. BARKER

Well, I certainly *look* a great deal more comfortable.

DADDY

I'm going to blush and giggle.

MOMMY

Daddy's going to blush and giggle.

MRS. BARKER

(Pulling the hem of her slip above her knees)
You're lucky to have such a man for a husband.

MOMMY

Oh, don't I know it!

DADDY

I just blushed and giggled and went sticky wet.

MOMMY

Isn't Daddy a caution, Mrs. Barker?

MRS. BARKER

Maybe if I smoked . . . ?

MOMMY

Oh, that isn't necessary.

MRS. BARKER

I don't mind if I do.

MOMMY

No; no, don't. Really.

MRS. BARKER

I don't mind . . .

MOMMY

I won't have you smoking in my house, and that's that! You're a professional woman.

DADDY

Grandma drinks AND smokes; don't you, Grandma?

GRANDMA

No.

MOMMY

Well, now, Mrs. Barker; suppose you tell us why you're here.

GRANDMA

(As MOMMY *walks through the boxes*)

The boxes . . . the boxes . . .

MOMMY

Be quiet, Grandma.

DADDY

What did you say, Grandma!

GRANDMA

(As MOMMY *steps on several of the boxes*)

The boxes, damn it!

MRS. BARKER

Boxes; she said boxes. She mentioned the boxes.

DADDY

What about the boxes, Grandma? Maybe Mrs. Barker is here because of the boxes. Is that what you meant, Grandma?

GRANDMA

I don't know if that's what I meant or not. It's certainly not what I *thought* I meant.

DADDY

Grandma is of the opinion that . . .

MRS. BARKER

Can we assume that the boxes are for us? I mean, can we assume that you had us come here for the boxes?

MOMMY

Are you in the habit of receiving boxes?

DADDY

A very good question.

MRS. BARKER

Well, that would depend on the reason we're here. I've got my fingers in so many little pies, you know. Now, I can think of one of my little activities in which we are in the habit of receiving *baskets;* but more in a literary sense than really. We *might* receive boxes, though, under very special circumstances. I'm afraid that's the best answer I can give you.

DADDY

It's a very interesting answer.

MRS. BARKER

I thought so. But, does it help?

MOMMY

No; I'm afraid not.

DADDY

I wonder if it might help us any if I said I feel misgivings, that I have definite qualms.

MOMMY

Where, Daddy?

DADDY

Well, mostly right here, right around where the stitches were.

MOMMY

Daddy had an operation, you know.

MRS. BARKER

Oh, you poor Daddy! I didn't know; but then, how could I?

GRANDMA

You might have asked; it wouldn't have hurt you.

MOMMY

Dry up, Grandma.

GRANDMA

There you go. Letting your true feelings come out. Old people aren't dry enough, I suppose. My sacks are empty, the fluid in my eyeballs is all caked on the inside edges, my spine is made of sugar candy, I breathe ice; but you don't hear me complain. Nobody hears old people complain because people think that's all old people do. And *that's* because old people are gnarled and sagged and twisted into the shape of a complaint.

(*Signs off*)

That's all.

MRS. BARKER

What was wrong, Daddy?

DADDY

Well, you know how it is: the doctors took out something that was there and put in something that wasn't there. An operation.

MRS. BARKER

You're very fortunate, I should say.

MOMMY

Oh, he is; he is. All his life, Daddy has wanted to be a United States Senator; but now . . . why now he's changed his mind, and for the rest of his life he's going to want to be Governor . . . it would be nearer the apartment, you know.

MRS. BARKER

You *are* fortunate, Daddy.

DADDY

Yes, indeed; except that I get these qualms now and then, definite ones.

MRS. BARKER

Well, it's just a matter of things settling; you're like an old house.

MOMMY

Why Daddy, thank Mrs. Barker.

DADDY

Thank you.

MRS. BARKER

Ambition! That's the ticket. I have a brother who's very much like you, Daddy . . . ambitious. Of course, he's a great deal younger than you; he's even younger than I am . . . if such a thing is possible. He runs a little newspaper. Just a little newspaper . . . but he runs it. He's chief cook and bottle washer of that little newspaper, which he calls *The Village Idiot.* He has such a sense of humor; he's so self-deprecating, so modest. And he'd never admit it himself, but he *is* the Village Idiot.

MOMMY

Oh, I think that's just grand. Don't you think so, Daddy?

DADDY

Yes, just grand.

MRS. BARKER

My brother's a dear man, and he has a dear little wife, whom he loves, dearly. He loves her so much he just can't get a sentence out without mentioning her. He wants everybody to know he's married. He's really a stickler on that point; he can't be introduced to anybody and say hello without adding, "Of course, I'm married." As far as I'm concerned, he's the chief exponent of Woman Love in this whole country; he's even been written up in psychiatric journals because of it.

DADDY

Indeed!

MOMMY

Isn't that lovely.

MRS. BARKER

Oh, I think so. There's too much woman hatred in this country, and that's a fact.

GRANDMA

Oh, I don't know.

MOMMY

Oh, I think that's just grand. Don't you think so, Daddy?

DADDY

Yes, just grand.

GRANDMA

In case anybody's interested . . .

MOMMY

Be quiet, Grandma.

GRANDMA

Nuts!

MOMMY

Oh, Mrs. Barker, you *must* forgive Grandma. She's rural.

MRS. BARKER

I don't mind if I do.

DADDY

Maybe Grandma has something to say.

MOMMY

Nonsense. Old people have nothing to say; and if old people *did* have something to say, nobody would listen to them.

(*To* GRANDMA)

You see? I can pull that stuff just as easy as you can.

GRANDMA

Well, you got the rhythm, but you don't really have the quality. Besides, you're middle-aged.

MOMMY

I'm proud of it!

GRANDMA

Look. I'll show you how it's really done. Middle-aged people think they can do anything, but the truth is that middle-aged people can't do most things as well as they used to. Middle-aged people think they're special because they're like everybody else. We live in the age of deformity. You see? Rhythm *and* content. You'll learn.

DADDY

I do wish I weren't surrounded by women; I'd like some men around here.

MRS. BARKER

You can say that again!

GRANDMA

I don't hardly count as a woman, so can I say my piece?

MOMMY

Go on. Jabber away.

GRANDMA

It's very simple; the fact is, these boxes don't have anything to do with why this good lady is come to call. Now, if you're interested in knowing why these boxes *are* here . . .

MOMMY

Well, nobody *is* interested!

GRANDMA

You can be as snippety as you like for all the good it'll do you.

DADDY

You two will have to stop arguing.

MOMMY

I don't argue with her.

DADDY

It will just have to stop.

MOMMY

Well, why don't you call a van and have her taken away?

GRANDMA

Don't bother; there's no need.

DADDY

No, now, perhaps I can go away myself. . . .

MOMMY

Well, one or the other; the way things are now it's impossible. In the first place, it's too crowded in this apartment.

(*To* GRANDMA)

And it's you that takes up all the space, with your enema bottles, and your Pekinese, and God-only-knows-what-else . . . and now all these boxes. . . .

GRANDMA

These boxes are . . .

MRS. BARKER

I've never heard of enema *bottles* . . .

GRANDMA

She means enema bags, but she doesn't know the difference. Mommy comes from extremely bad stock. And besides, when Mommy was born . . . well, it was a difficult delivery, and she had a head shaped like a banana.

) *HAHA*

MOMMY

You ungrateful—Daddy? Daddy, you see how ungrateful she is after all these years, after all the things we've done for her?

(*To* GRANDMA)

One of these days you're going away in a van; that's what's going to happen to you!

GRANDMA

Do tell!

MRS. BARKER

Like a banana?

GRANDMA

Yup, just like a banana.

MRS. BARKER

My word!

MOMMY

You stop listening to her; she'll say anything. just the other night she called Daddy a hedgehog.

MRS. BARKER

She didn't!

GRANDMA

That's right, baby; you stick up for me.

MOMMY

I don't know where she gets the words; on the television, maybe.

MRS. BARKER

Did you really call him a hedgehog?

GRANDMA

Oh look; what difference does it make whether I did or not?

DADDY

Grandma's right. Leave Grandma alone.

MOMMY

(To DADDY)
How dare you!

GRANDMA

Oh, leave her alone, Daddy; the kid's all mixed up.

MOMMY

You see? I told you. It's all those television shows. Daddy, you go right into Grandma's room and take her television and shake all the tubes loose.

DADDY

Don't mention tubes to me.

MOMMY

Oh! Mommy forgot!
   (*To* MRS. BARKER)
Daddy has tubes now, where he used to have tracts.

MRS. BARKER

Is that a fact!

GRANDMA

I know why this dear lady is here.

MOMMY

You be still.

MRS. BARKER

Oh, I do wish you'd tell me.

MOMMY

No! No! That wouldn't be fair at all.

DADDY

Besides, she knows why she's here; she's here because we called
them.

MRS. BARKER

La! But that still leaves me puzzled. I know I'm here because you
called us, but I'm such a busy girl, with this committee and that
committee, and the Responsible Citizens Activities I indulge in.

MOMMY

Oh my; busy, busy.

MRS. BARKER

Yes, indeed. So I'm afraid you'll have to give me some help.

MOMMY

Oh, no. No, you must be mistaken. I can't believe we asked you here
to give you any help. With the way taxes are these days, and the way
you can't get satisfaction in ANYTHING . . . no, I don't believe so.

DADDY

And if you need help . . . why, I should think you'd apply for a
Fulbright Scholarship. . . .

MOMMY

And if not that . . . why, then a Guggenheim Fellowship. . . .

GRANDMA

Oh, come on; why not shoot the works and try for the Prix de Rome.

(*Under her breath to* MOMMY *and* DADDY)

Beasts!

MRS. BARKER

Oh, what a jolly family. But let me think. I'm knee-deep in work these days; there's the Ladies' Auxiliary Air Raid Committee, for one thing; how do you feel about air raids?

MOMMY

Oh, I'd say we're hostile.

DADDY

Yes, definitely; we're hostile.

MRS. BARKER

Then, you'll be no help there. There's too much hostility in the world these days as it is; but I'll not badger you! There's a surfeit of badgers as well.

GRANDMA

While we're at it, there's been a run on old people, too. The Department of Agriculture, or maybe it wasn't the Department of Agriculture—anyway, it was some department that's run by a girl— put out figures showing that ninety per cent of the adult population of the country is over eighty years old . . . or eighty per cent is over ninety years old . . .

MOMMY

You're such a liar! You just finished saying that everyone is middle-aged.

GRANDMA

I'm just telling you what the government says . . . that doesn't have anything to do with what . . .

MOMMY

It's that television! Daddy, go break her television.

GRANDMA

You won't find it.

DADDY

(Wearily getting up)
If I must . . . I must.

MOMMY

And don't step on the Pekinese; it's blind.

DADDY

It may be blind, but Daddy isn't.
(He exits, through the archway, stage-left)

GRANDMA

You won't find *it*, either.

MOMMY

Oh, I'm so fortunate to have such a husband. Just think: I could
have a husband who was poor, or argumentative, or a husband who
sat in a wheelchair all day . . . OOOOHHHH! *What* have I said? What
have I said?

GRANDMA

You said you could have a husband who sat in a wheel . . .

MOMMY

I'm mortified! I could die! I could cut my tongue out! I could . . .

MRS. BARKER

(Forcing a smile)
Oh, now . . . now . . . don't think about it . . .

MOMMY

I could . . . why, I could . . .

MRS. BARKER

. . . don't think about it . . . really . . .

MOMMY

You're quite right. I won't think about it, and that way I'll forget that
I ever said it, and that way it will be all right.
(Pause)
There . . . I've forgotten. Well, now, now that Daddy is out of the
room we can have some girl talk.

MRS. BARKER

I'm not sure that I . . .

MOMMY

You *do* want to have some girl talk, don't you?

MRS. BARKER

I was going to say I'm not sure that I wouldn't care for a glass of water. I feel a little faint.

MOMMY

Grandma, go get Mrs. Barker a glass of water.

GRANDMA

Go get it yourself. I quit.

MOMMY

Grandma loves to do little things around the house; it gives her a false sense of security.

GRANDMA

I quit! I'm through!

MOMMY

Now, you be a good Grandma, or you know what will happen to you. You'll be taken away in a van.

GRANDMA

You don't frighten me. I'm too old to be frightened. Besides . . .

MOMMY

WELL! I'll tend to you later. I'll hide your teeth . . . I'll . . .

GRANDMA

Everything's hidden.

MRS. BARKER

I *am* going to faint. I *am.*

MOMMY

Good heavens! I'll go myself.
      (*As she exits, through the archway, stage-left*)
I'll fix you, Grandma. I'll take care of you later.
      (*She exits*)

GRANDMA

Oh, go soak your head.

(*To* MRS. BARKER)

Well, dearie, how do you feel?

MRS. BARKER

A little better, I think. Yes, much better, thank you, Grandma.

GRANDMA

That's good.

MRS. BARKER

But . . . I feel so lost . . . not knowing why I'm here . . . and, on top of it, they say I was here before.

GRANDMA

Well, you were. You weren't *here*, exactly, because we've moved around a lot, from one apartment to another, up and down the social ladder like mice, if you like similes.

MRS. BARKER

I don't . . . particularly.

GRANDMA

Well, then, I'm sorry.

MRS. BARKER

(*Suddenly*)

Grandma, I feel I can trust you.

GRANDMA

Don't be too sure; it's every man for himself around this place. . . .

MRS. BARKER

Oh . . . is it? Nonetheless, I really do feel that I can trust you. *Please* tell me why they called and asked us to come.

GRANDMA

Well, I'll give you a hint. That's the best I can do, because I'm a muddleheaded old woman. Now listen, because it's important. Once upon a time, not too very long ago, but a long enough time ago . . . oh, about twenty years ago . . . there was a man very much like Daddy, and a woman very much like Mommy, who were married to each other, very much like Mommy and Daddy are married to each other; and they lived in an apartment very much like one that's very much like this one, and they lived there with an old woman who was very much like yours truly, only younger, because it was some time ago; in fact, they were all somewhat younger.

MRS. BARKER

How fascinating!

GRANDMA

Now, at the same time, there was a dear lady very much like you, only younger then, who did all sorts of Good Works. . . . And one of the Good Works this dear lady did was in something very much like a volunteer capacity for an organization very much like the Bye-Bye Adoption Service, which is nearby and which was run by a terribly deaf old lady very much like the Miss Bye-Bye who runs the Bye-Bye Adoption Service nearby.

MRS. BARKER

How enthralling!

GRANDMA

Well, be that as it may. Nonetheless, one afternoon this man, who was very much like Daddy, and this woman who was very much like Mommy came to see this dear lady who did all the Good Works, who was very much like you, dear, and they were very sad and very hopeful, and they cried and smiled and bit their fingers, and they said all the most intimate things.

MRS. BARKER

How spellbinding! What did they say?

GRANDMA

Well, it was very sweet. The woman, who was very much like Mommy, said that she and the man who was very much like Daddy had never been blessed with anything very much like a bumble of joy.

MRS. BARKER

A what?

GRANDMA

A bumble; a bumble of joy.

MRS. BARKER

Oh, like bundle.

GRANDMA

Well, yes; very much like it. Bundle, bumble; who cares? At any rate, the woman, who was very much like Mommy, said that they wanted a bumble of their own, but that the man, who was very much like Daddy, couldn't have a bumble; and the man, who was very much like Daddy, said that yes, they had wanted a bumble of their own, but that the woman, who was very much like Mommy, couldn't have one, and that now they wanted to buy something very much like a bumble.

MRS. BARKER

How engrossing!

GRANDMA

Yes. And the dear lady, who was very much like you, said something that was very much like, "Oh, what a shame; but take heart . . . I think we have just the bumble *for* you." And, well, the lady, who was very much like Mommy, and the man, who was very much like Daddy, cried and smiled and bit their fingers, and said some more intimate things, which were totally irrelevant but which were pretty hot stuff, and so the dear lady, who was very much like you, and who had something very much like a penchant for pornography, listened with something very much like enthusiasm. "Whee," she said. "Whoooopeeeeee!" But that's beside the point.

MRS. BARKER

I suppose *so*. But how gripping!

GRANDMA

Anyway . . . they *bought* something very much like a bumble, and they took it away with them. But . . . things didn't work out very well.

MRS. BARKER

You mean there was trouble?

GRANDMA

You got it.
   (With a glance through the archway)
But, I'm going to have to speed up now because I think I'm leaving soon.

MRS. BARKER

Oh. Are you really?

GRANDMA

Yup.

MRS. BARKER

But old people don't go anywhere; they're either taken places, or put places.

GRANDMA

Well, this old person is different. Anyway . . . things started going badly.

MRS. BARKER

Oh yes. Yes.

GRANDMA

Weeeeellll . . . in the first place, it turned out the bumble didn't look like either one of its parents. That was enough of a blow, but things got worse. One night, it cried its heart out, if you can imagine such a thing.

MRS. BARKER

Cried its heart out! Well!

GRANDMA

But that was only the beginning. Then it turned out it only had eyes for its Daddy.

MRS. BARKER

For its Daddy! Why, any self-respecting woman would have gouged those eyes right out of its head.

GRANDMA

Well, she did. That's exactly what she did. But then, it kept its nose up in the air.

MRS. BARKER

Ufggh! How disgusting!

GRANDMA

That's what they thought. But *then,* it began to develop an interest in its you-know-what.

MRS. BARKER

In its you-know-what! Well! I hope they cut its hands off at the wrists!

GRANDMA

Well, yes, they did that eventually. But first, they cut off its you-
know-what.

MRS. BARKER

A much better idea!

GRANDMA

That's what they thought. But after they cut off its you-know-what,
it *still* put its hands under the covers, *looking* for its you-know-what.
So, finally, they *had* to cut off its hands at the wrists.

MRS. BARKER

Naturally!

GRANDMA

And it was such a resentful bumble. Why, one day it called its
Mommy a dirty name.

MRS. BARKER

Well, I hope they cut its tongue out!

GRANDMA

Of course. And then, as it got bigger, they found out all sorts of terrible things about it, like: it didn't have a head on its shoulders, it had
no guts, it was spineless, its feet were made of clay . . . just dreadful
things.

MRS. BARKER

Dreadful!

GRANDMA

So you can understand how they became discouraged.

MRS. BARKER

I certainly can! And what did they do?

GRANDMA

What did they do? Well, for the last straw, it finally up and died; and
you can imagine how *that* made them feel, their having paid for it,
and all. So, they called up the lady who sold them the bumble in the
first place and told her to come right over to their apartment. They
wanted satisfaction; they wanted their money back. That's what they
wanted.

MRS. BARKER

My, my, my.

GRANDMA

How do you like *them* apples?

MRS. BARKER

My, my, my.

DADDY

(*Off stage*)

Mommy! I can't find Grandma's television, and I can't find the Pekinese, either.

MOMMY

(*Off stage*)

Isn't that funny! And I can't find the water.

GRANDMA

Heh, heh, heh. I told them everything was hidden.

MRS. BARKER

Did you hide the water, too?

GRANDMA

(*Puzzled*)

No. No, I didn't do *that*.

DADDY

(*Off stage*)

The truth of the matter is, I can't even find Grandma's room.

GRANDMA

Heh, heh, heh.

MRS. BARKER

My! You certainly did hide things, didn't you?

GRANDMA

Sure, kid, sure.

MOMMY

(*Sticking her head in the room*)

Did you ever hear of such a thing, Grandma? Daddy can't find your television, and he can't find the Pekinese, and the truth of the matter is he can't even find your room.

GRANDMA

I told you. I hid everything.

MOMMY

Nonsense, Grandma! Just wait until I get my hands on you. You're a
troublemaker . . . that's what you are.

GRANDMA

Well, I'll be out of here pretty soon, baby.

MOMMY

Oh, you don't know how right you are! Daddy's been wanting to
send you away for a long time now, but I've been restraining him.
I'll tell you one thing, though . . . I'm getting sick and tired of this
fighting, and I might just let him have his way. Then you'll see
what'll happen. Away you'll go; in a van, too. I'll let Daddy call the
van man.

GRANDMA

I'm way ahead of you.

MOMMY

How can you be so old and so smug at the same time? You have no
sense of proportion.

GRANDMA

You just answered your own question.

MOMMY

Mrs. Barker, I'd much rather you came into the kitchen for that glass
of water, what with Grandma out here, and all.

MRS. BARKER

I don't see what Grandma has to do with it; and besides, I don't think
you're very polite.

MOMMY

You seem to forget that you're a guest in this house . . .

GRANDMA

Apartment!

MOMMY

Apartment! And that you're a professional woman. So, if you'll be so
good as to come into the kitchen, I'll be more than happy to show

you where the water is, and where the glass is, and then you can put
two and two together, if you're clever enough.

(She vanishes)

MRS. BARKER

(After a moment's consideration)

I suppose she's right.

GRANDMA

Well, that's how it is when people call you up and ask you over to do
something for them.

MRS. BARKER

I suppose you're right, too. Well, Grandma, it's been very nice talking to you.

GRANDMA

And I've enjoyed listening. Say, don't tell Mommy or Daddy that I
gave you that hint, will you?

MRS. BARKER

Oh, dear me, the hint! I'd forgotten about it, if you can imagine such
a thing. No, I won't breathe a word of it to them.

GRANDMA

I don't know if it helped you any . . .

MRS. BARKER

I can't tell, yet. I'll have to . . . what *is* the word I want? . . . I'll
have to relate it . . . that's it . . . I'll have to relate it to certain
things that I *know,* and . . . draw . . . conclusions. . . . What I'll
really have to do is to see if it applies to anything. I mean, after
all, I *do* do volunteer work for an adoption service, but it isn't
very much *like* the Bye-Bye Adoption Service . . . it *is* the Bye-
Bye Adoption Service . . . and while I can remember Mommy and
Daddy coming to see me, oh about twenty years ago, about buying a bumble, I can't quite remember anyone very much *like*
Mommy and Daddy coming to see me about buying a bumble.
Don't you see? It really presents quite a problem. . . . I'll have to
think about it . . . mull it . . . but at any rate, it was truly first-class
of you to try to help me. Oh, will you still be here after I've had
my drink of water?

GRANDMA

Probably . . . I'm not as spry as I used to be.

MRS. BARKER

Oh. Well, I won't say good-by then.

GRANDMA

No. Don't.

(MRS. BARKER *exits through the archway*)

People don't say good-by to old people because they think they'll frighten them. Lordy! If they only knew how awful "hello" and "my, you're looking chipper" sounded, they wouldn't say those things either. The truth is, there isn't much you *can* say to old people that doesn't sound just terrible.

(*The doorbell rings*)

Come on in!

(*The* YOUNG MAN *enters.* GRANDMA *looks him over*)

Well, now, aren't you a breath of fresh air!

YOUNG MAN

Hello there.

GRANDMA

My, my, my. Are you the van man?

YOUNG MAN

The what?

GRANDMA

The van man. The van man. Are you come to take me away?

YOUNG MAN

I don't know what you're talking about.

GRANDMA

Oh.

(*Pause*)

Well.

(*Pause*)

My, my, aren't you something!

YOUNG MAN

Hm?

GRANDMA

, my, my, aren't you something.

YOUNG MAN

Oh. Thank you.

GRANDMA

You don't sound very enthusiastic.

YOUNG MAN

Oh, I'm . . . I'm used to it.

GRANDMA

Yup . . . yup. You know, if I were about a hundred and fifty years younger I could go for you.

YOUNG MAN

Yes, I imagine so.

GRANDMA

Unh-hunh . . . will you look at those muscles!

YOUNG MAN

(Flexing his muscles)

Yes, they're quite good, aren't they?

GRANDMA

Boy, they sure are. They natural?

YOUNG MAN

Well the basic structure was there, but I've done some work, too . . . you know, in a gym.

GRANDMA

I'll bet you have. You ought to be in the movies, boy.

YOUNG MAN

I know.

GRANDMA

Yup! Right up there on the old silver screen. But I suppose you've heard that before.

YOUNG MAN

Yes, I have.

GRANDMA

You ought to try out for them . . . the movies.

YOUNG MAN

Well, actually, I may have a career there yet. I've lived out on the West Coast almost all my life . . . and I've met a few people who . . . might be able to help me. I'm not in too much of a hurry, though. I'm almost as young as I look.

GRANDMA

Oh, that's nice. And will you look at that face!

YOUNG MAN

Yes, it's quite good, isn't it? Clean-cut, Midwest farm boy type, almost insultingly good-looking in a typically American way. Good profile, straight nose, honest eyes, wonderful smile . . .

GRANDMA

Yup. Boy, you know what you are, don't you? You're the American Dream, that's what you are. All those other people, they don't know what they're talking about. You . . . *you* are the American Dream.

YOUNG MAN

Thanks.

MOMMY

(Off stage)
Who rang the doorbell?

GRANDMA

(Shouting off stage)
The American Dream!

MOMMY

(Off stage)
What? What was that, Grandma?

GRANDMA

(Shouting)
The American Dream! The American Dream! Damn it!

DADDY

(Off stage)
How's that, Mommy?

MOMMY

(Off stage)

Oh, some gibberish; pay no attention. Did you find Grandma's room?

DADDY

(Off stage)

No. I can't even find Mrs. Barker.

YOUNG MAN

What was all that?

GRANDMA

Oh, that was just the folks, but let's not talk about them, honey; let's talk about you.

YOUNG MAN

All right.

GRANDMA

Well, let's see. If you're not the van man, what are you doing here?

YOUNG MAN

I'm looking for work.

GRANDMA

Are you! Well, what kind of work?

YOUNG MAN

Oh, almost anything . . . almost anything that pays. I'll do almost anything for money.

GRANDMA

Will you . . . will you? Hmmmm. I wonder if there's anything you could do around here?

YOUNG MAN

There might be. It looked to be a likely building.

GRANDMA

It's always looked to be a rather unlikely building to me, but I suppose you'd know better than I.

YOUNG MAN

I can sense these things.

GRANDMA

There *might* be something you could do around here. Stay there!
Don't come any closer.

YOUNG MAN

Sorry.

GRANDMA

I don't mean I'd *mind.* I don't know whether I'd mind, or not. . . .
But it wouldn't look well; it would look just *awful.*

YOUNG MAN

Yes; I suppose so.

GRANDMA

Now, stay there, let me concentrate. What could you do? The folks
have been in something of a quandary around here today, sort of a
dilemma, and I wonder if you mightn't be some help.

YOUNG MAN

I hope so . . . if there's money in it. Do you have any money?

GRANDMA

Money! Oh, there's more money around here than you'd know what
to do with.

YOUNG MAN

I'm not so sure.

GRANDMA

Well, maybe not. Besides, I've got money of my own.

YOUNG MAN

You have?

GRANDMA

Sure. Old people quite often have lots of money; more often than
most people expect. Come here, so I can whisper to you . . . not too
close. I might faint.

YOUNG MAN

Oh, I'm sorry.

GRANDMA

It's all right, dear. Anyway . . . have you ever heard of that big baking contest they run? The one where all the ladies get together in a
big barn and bake away?

YOUNG MAN

I'm . . . not . . . sure. . . .

GRANDMA

Not so close. Well, it doesn't matter whether you've heard of it or
not. The important thing is—and I don't want anybody to hear this
. . . the folks think I haven't been out of the house in eight years—
the important thing is that I won first prize in that baking contest
this year. Oh, it was in all the papers; not under my own name,
though. I used a *nom de boulangère;* I called myself Uncle Henry.

YOUNG MAN

Did you?

GRANDMA

Why not? I didn't see any reason not to. I look just as much like an
old man as I do like an old woman. And you know what I called it
. . . what I won for?

YOUNG MAN

No. What did you call it?

GRANDMA

I called it Uncle Henry's Day-Old Cake.

YOUNG MAN

That's a very nice name.

GRANDMA

And it wasn't any trouble, either. All I did was go out and get a store-
bought cake, and keep it around for a while, and then slip it in,
unbeknownst to anybody. Simple.

YOUNG MAN

You're a very resourceful person.

GRANDMA

Pioneer stock.

YOUNG MAN

Is all this true? Do you want me to believe all this?

GRANDMA

Well, you can believe it or not . . . it doesn't make any difference to
me. All *I* know is, Uncle Henry's Day-Old Cake won me twenty-five
thousand smackerolas.

YOUNG MAN

Twenty-five thou—

GRANDMA

Right on the old loggerhead. Now . . . how do you like them apples?

YOUNG MAN

Love 'em.

GRANDMA

I thought you'd be impressed.

YOUNG MAN

Money talks.

GRANDMA

Hey! You look familiar.

YOUNG MAN

Hm? Pardon?

GRANDMA

I said, you look familiar.

YOUNG MAN

Well, I've done some modeling.

GRANDMA

No . . . no. I don't mean that. You look familiar.

YOUNG MAN

Well, I'm a type.

GRANDMA

Yup; you sure are. Why do you say you'd do almost anything for
money . . . if you don't mind my being nosy?

YOUNG MAN

No, no. It's part of the interview. I'll be happy to tell you. It's that
I have no talents at all, except what you see . . . my person; my body,
my face. In every other way I am incomplete, and I must therefore
. . . compensate.

GRANDMA

at do you mean, incomplete? You look pretty complete to me.

YOUNG MAN

I think I can explain it to you, partially because you're very old, and very old people have perceptions they keep to themselves, because if they expose them to other people . . . well, you know what ridicule and neglect are.

GRANDMA

I do, child, I do.

YOUNG MAN

Then listen. My mother died the night that I was born, and I never knew my father; I doubt my mother did. But, I wasn't alone, because lying with me . . . in the placenta . . . there was someone else . . . my brother . . . my twin.

GRANDMA

Oh, my child.

YOUNG MAN

We were identical twins . . . he and I . . . not fraternal . . . identical; we were derived from the same ovum; and in *this,* in that we were twins not from separate ova but from the same one, we had a kinship such as you cannot imagine. We . . . we felt each other breathe . . . his heartbeats thundered in my temples . . . mine in his . . . our stomachs ached and we cried for feeding at the same time . . . are you old enough to understand?

GRANDMA

I think so, child; I think I'm nearly old enough.

YOUNG MAN

I hope so. But we were separated when we were still very young, my brother, my twin and I . . . inasmuch as you can separate one being. We were torn apart . . . thrown to opposite ends of the continent. I don't know what became of my brother . . . to the rest of myself . . . except that, from time to time, in the years that have passed, I have suffered losses . . . that I can't explain. A fall from grace . . . a departure of innocence . . . loss. . . . loss. How can I put it to you? All right; like this: Once . . . it was as if all at once my heart . . . became numb . . . almost as though I . . . almost as

though . . . just like that . . . it had been wrenched from my body
. . . and from that time I have been unable to love. Once . . . I was
asleep at the time . . . I awoke, and my eyes were burning. And
since that time I have been unable to see anything, *anything,* with
pity, with affection . . . with anything but . . . cool disinterest. And
my groin . . . even there . . . since one time . . . one specific agony
. . . since then I have not been able to *love* anyone with my body.
And even my hands . . . I cannot touch another person and feel love.
And there is more . . . there are more losses, but it all comes down
to this: I no longer have the capacity to feel anything. I have no
emotions. I have been drained, torn asunder . . . disemboweled. I
have, now, only my person . . . my body, my face. I use what I have
. . . I let people love me . . . I accept the syntax around me, for
while I know I cannot relate . . . I know I must be related *to.* I let
people love me . . . I let people touch me . . . I let them draw pleasure from my groin . . . from my presence . . . from the fact of me
. . . but, that is all it comes to. As I told you, I am incomplete . . .
I can feel nothing. I can feel nothing. And so . . . here I am . . . as
you see me. I am . . . but this . . . what you see. And it will always
be thus.

GRANDMA

Oh, my child; my child.

(Long pause; then)

I was mistaken . . . before. I don't know you from somewhere, but I
knew . . . once . . . someone very much like you . . . or, very much as
perhaps you were.

YOUNG MAN

Be careful; be very careful. What I have told you may not be true.
In my profession . . .

GRANDMA

Shhhhhh.

(The YOUNG MAN *bows his head, in acquiescence)*

Someone . . . to be more precise . . . who might have turned out to
be very much like you might have turned out to be. And . . . unless
I'm terribly mistaken . . . you've found yourself a job.

YOUNG MAN

What are my duties?

MRS. BARKER

(*Off stage*)
Yoo-hoo! Yoo-hoo!

GRANDMA

Oh-oh. You'll . . . you'll have to play it by ear, my dear . . . unless I
get a chance to talk to you again. I've got to go into my act, now.

YOUNG MAN

But, I . . .

GRANDMA

Yoo-hoo!

MRS. BARKER

(*Coming through archway*)
Yoo-hoo . . . oh, there you are, Grandma. I'm glad to see somebody.
I can't find Mommy or Daddy.
    (*Double takes*)
Well . . . who's this?

GRANDMA

This? Well . . . uh . . . oh, this is the . . . uh . . . the van man. That's
who it is . . . the van man.

MRS. BARKER

So! It's true! They *did* call the van man. They *are* having you carted
away.

GRANDMA

(*Shrugging*)
Well, you know. It figures.

MRS. BARKER

(*To* YOUNG MAN)
How dare you cart this poor old woman away!

YOUNG MAN

(*After a quick look at* GRANDMA, *who nods*)
I do what I'm paid to do. I don't ask any questions.

MRS. BARKER

(*After a brief pause*)
Oh.

(Pause)

Well, you're quite right, of course, and I shouldn't meddle.

GRANDMA

(To YOUNG MAN*)*

Dear, will you take my things out to the van?

(She points to the boxes)

YOUNG MAN

(After only the briefest hesitation)

Why certainly.

GRANDMA

(As the YOUNG MAN *takes up half the boxes, exits by the front door)*

Isn't that a nice young van man?

MRS. BARKER

(Shaking her head in disbelief, watching the YOUNG MAN *exit)*

Unh-hunh . . . some things have changed for the better. I remember when I had *my* mother carted off . . . the van man who came for her wasn't anything near as nice as this one.

GRANDMA

Oh, did you have your mother carted off, too?

MRS. BARKER *(Cheerfully)*

Why certainly! Didn't you?

GRANDMA *(Puzzling)*   — a new development

No . . . no, I didn't. At least, I can't remember. Listen dear; I got to talk to you for a second.

MRS. BARKER

Why certainly, Grandma.

GRANDMA

Now, listen.

MRS. BARKER

Yes, Grandma. Yes.

GRANDMA
Now listen carefully. You got this dilemma here with Mommy and Daddy . . .

MRS. BARKER
Yes! I wonder where they've gone to.

GRANDMA
They'll be back in. Now, LISTEN!

MRS. BARKER
Oh, I'm sorry.

GRANDMA
Now, you got this dilemma here with Mommy and Daddy, and I think I got the way out for you.
(The YOUNG MAN *re-enters through the front door)*
Will you take the rest of my things out now, dear?
(To MRS. BARKER, *while the* YOUNG MAN *takes the rest of the boxes, exits again by the front door)*
Fine. Now listen, dear.
(She begins to whisper in MRS. BARKER's *ear)*

MRS. BARKER
Oh! Oh! Oh! I don't think I could . . . do you really think I could? Well, why not? What a wonderful idea . . . what an absolutely wonderful idea!

GRANDMA
Well, yes, I thought it was.

MRS. BARKER
And you so old!

GRANDMA
Heh, heh, heh.

MRS. BARKER
Well, I think it's absolutely marvelous, anyway. I'm going to find Mommy and Daddy right now.

GRANDMA
Good. You do that.

MRS. BARKER

Well, now. I think I will say good-by. I can't thank you enough.

(She starts to exit through the archway)

GRANDMA

You're welcome. Say it!

MRS. BARKER

Huh? What?

GRANDMA

Say good-by.

MRS. BARKER

Oh. Good-by.

(She exits)

Mommy! I say, Mommy! Daddy!

GRANDMA

Good-by.

(By herself now, she looks about)

Ah me.

(Shakes her head)

Ah me.

(Takes in the room)

Good-by.

(The YOUNG MAN *re-enters)*

Oh, hello, there.

YOUNG MAN

All the boxes are outside.

GRANDMA

(A little sadly)

I don't know why I bother to take them with me. They don't have
much in them . . . some old letters, a couple of regrets . . . Pekinese
. . . blind at that . . . the television . . . my Sunday teeth . . . eighty-
six years of living . . . some sounds . . . a few images, a little garbled
by now . . . and, well . . .

(She shrugs)

. . . you know . . . the things one accumulates.

YOUNG MAN

Can I get you . . . a cab, or something?

GRANDMA

Oh no, dear . . . thank you just the same. I'll take it from here.

YOUNG MAN

And what shall I do now?

GRANDMA

Oh, you stay here, dear. It will all become clear to you. It will be explained. You'll understand.

YOUNG MAN

Very well.

GRANDMA

(After one more look about)

Well . . .

YOUNG MAN

Let me see you to the elevator.

GRANDMA

Oh . . . that *would* be nice, dear.

(They both exit by the front door, slowly)

(Enter MRS. BARKER, *followed by* MOMMY *and* DADDY*)*

MRS. BARKER

. . . and I'm happy to tell you that the whole thing's settled. Just like that.

MOMMY

Oh, we're so glad. We were afraid there might be a problem, what with delays, and all.

DADDY

Yes, we re very relieved.

MRS. BARKER

Well, now; that's what professional women are for.

MOMMY

Why . . . where's Grandma? Grandma's not here! Where's Grandma? And look! The boxes are gone, too. Grandma's gone, and so are the boxes. She's taken off and she's stolen something! Daddy!

MRS. BARKER

Why, Mommy, the van man was here.

MOMMY

(Startled)

The what?

MRS. BARKER

The van man. The van man was here.

(The lights might dim a little, suddenly)

MOMMY

(Shakes her head)

No, that's impossible.

MRS. BARKER

Why, I saw him with my own two eyes.

MOMMY

(Near tears)

No, no, that's impossible. No. There's no such thing as the van man. There is no van man. We . . . we made him up. Grandma? Grandma?

DADDY

(Moving to MOMMY)

There, there, now.

MOMMY

Oh Daddy . . . where's Grandma?

DADDY

There, there, now.

(While DADDY is comforting MOMMY, GRANDMA comes out, stage right, near the footlights)

GRANDMA

(To the audience)

Shhhhhh! I want to watch this.

(She motions to MRS. BARKER, who, with a secret smile, tip-toes to the front door and opens it. The YOUNG MAN is framed therein. Lights up full again as he steps into the room)

MRS. BARKER

Surprise! Surprise! Here we are!

MOMMY

What? What?

DADDY

Hm? What?

MOMMY

(Her tears merely sniffles now)

What surprise?

MRS. BARKER

Why, I told you. The surprise I told you about.

DADDY

You . . . you know, Mommy.

MOMMY

Sur . . . prise?

DADDY

(Urging her to cheerfulness)

You remember, Mommy; why we asked . . . uh . . . what's-her-name
to come here?

MRS. BARKER

Mrs. Barker, if you don't mind.

DADDY

Yes. Mommy? You remember now? About the bumble . . . about
wanting satisfaction?

MOMMY

(Her sorrow turning into delight)

Yes. Why yes! Of course! Yes! Oh, how wonderful!

MRS. BARKER

(To the YOUNG MAN)

This is Mommy.

YOUNG MAN

How . . . how do you do?

MRS. BARKER

(*Stage whisper*)
Her name's Mommy.

YOUNG MAN

How . . . how do you do, Mommy?

MOMMY

Well! Hello there!

MRS. BARKER

(*To the* YOUNG MAN)
And that is Daddy.

YOUNG MAN

How do you do, sir?

DADDY

How do you do?

MOMMY

(*Herself again, circling the young man, feeling his arm, poking him*)
Yes, sir! Yes, sirree! Now this is more like it. Now this is a great deal
more like it! Daddy! Come see. Come see if this isn't a great deal
more like it.

DADDY

I . . . I can see from here, Mommy. It does look a great deal more
like it.

MOMMY

Yes, sir. Yes sirree! Mrs. Barker, I don't know *how* to thank you.

MRS. BARKER

Oh, don't worry about that. I'll send you a bill in the mail.

MOMMY

What this really calls for is a celebration. It calls for a drink.

MRS. BARKER

Oh, what a nice idea.

MOMMY

There's some sauterne in the kitchen.

YOUNG MAN

I'll go.

MOMMY

Will you? Oh, how nice. The kitchen's through the archway there.
(As the YOUNG MAN *exits: to* MRS. BARKER*)*
He's very nice. Really top notch; much better than the other one.

MRS. BARKER

I'm glad you're pleased. And I'm glad everything's all straightened
out.

MOMMY

Well, at least we know why we sent for you. We're glad that's cleared
up. By the way, what's his name?

MRS. BARKER

Ha! Call him whatever you like. He's yours. Call him what you called
the other one.

MOMMY

Daddy? What did we call the other one?

DADDY

(Puzzles)
Why . . .

YOUNG MAN

*(Re-entering with a tray on which are a bottle of sauterne
and five glasses)*
Here we are!

MOMMY

Hooray! Hooray!

MRS. BARKER

Oh, good!

MOMMY

(Moving to the tray)
So, let's— Five glasses? Why five? There are only four of us. Why
five?

YOUNG MAN

(Catches GRANDMA's *eye;* GRANDMA *indicates she is not there)*

Oh, I'm sorry.

MOMMY

You must learn to count. We're a wealthy family, and you must learn to count.

YOUNG MAN

I will.

MOMMY

Well, everybody take a glass.

(They do)

And we'll drink to celebrate. To satisfaction! Who says you can't get satisfaction these days!

MRS. BARKER

What dreadful sauterne!

MOMMY

Yes, isn't it?

(To YOUNG MAN, *her voice already a little fuzzy from the wine)*

You don't know how happy I am to see you! Yes sirree. Listen, that time we had with . . . with the other one. I'll tell you about it some time.

(Indicates MRS. BARKER*)*

I'll tell you all about it.

(Sidles up to him a little)

Maybe . . . maybe later tonight.

YOUNG MAN

(Not moving away)

Why yes. That would be very nice.

MOMMY

(Puzzles)

Something familiar about you . . . you know that? I can't quite place it. . . .

GRANDMA

(Interrupting . . . to audience)

Well, I guess that just about wraps it up. I mean, for better or worse, this is a comedy, and I don't think we'd better go any further. No, definitely not. So, let's leave things as they are right now . . . while everybody's happy . . . while everybody's got what he wants . . . or everybody's got what he thinks he wants. Good night, dears.

CURTAIN